THE
WIMBLEDON
MISCELLANY

SPENCER VIGNES

For Luca

First published 2010

The History Press
The Mill, Brimscombe Port
Stroud, Gloucestershire, GL5 2QG
www.thehistorypress.co.uk

British Library Cataloguing in Publication Data.
A catalogue record for this book is available from the British Library.

ISBN 978 0 7524 5560 0
Typesetting and origination by The History Press
Printed in Great Britain
Manufacturing managed by Jellyfish Print Solutions Ltd

FOREWORD

By Des Lynam OBE

I first went to the Wimbledon Championships at the age of 15, when as this book reminds us, the Men's final was played on Fridays, and immediately became entranced with the place, its traditions and history. I couldn't possibly have dreamt then that one day I would not only commentate on the championships for radio but actually present them for BBC television.

Like me the author first went there as a boy and has had a continuing love affair with Wimbledon ever since. This will become obvious over the pages to come as he delves into the beginnings of the event and brings us right up to date with tales that you may never have imagined and facts that have passed you by, all delivered with care and a lightness of touch.

For example, would you know who the first player was to be disqualified from Wimbledon? Connors, McEnroe, Nastase might all spring to mind. The answer is a big surprise.

We're reminded of the incredible sportsmanship of Britain's Roger Taylor and my old colleague the legendary commentator Dan Maskell, who mostly got it right but not always. I like his, 'When Martina's tense it helps her relax,' or, 'The Gullikson twins, both from Wisconsin.'

If you love tennis and you love Wimbledon then this book will be a joy.

ACKNOWLEDGEMENTS

First, a big tip of the hat to those who have gone before me. Just about all of what follows has been taken from my own notes, made over the course of many years working as a journalist. However, a fair chunk of those notes were originally sourced from articles and books written by the likes of Reg Brace, Alan Little, Laurie Pignon, Lance Tingay, Peter Wilson and others who were busy chronicling tennis long before I was even born. Thank you, gentlemen, for doing what you did and inspiring me to follow in your footsteps. This book would not have been possible without the patience and understanding of my children Rhiannon and Luca (for staying out of my way during the writing process) and partner Jane (likewise, plus providing mugs of tea and checking the occasional spelling). Last but not least thanks to Michelle Tilling at The History Press whose idea this was in the first place. It's been a blast!

Spencer Vignes

THE MISCELLANY

IN THE BEGINNING

Legend has it that the inaugural Championships of The All England Lawn Tennis and Croquet Club were held in order to raise money to repair the club's pony roller, the one used to maintain the croquet lawns. Then again comedian Billy Connolly once said that legend is nothing more than rumour plus time, so make of that what you will. What is for sure is that the very first Championships got underway at around 3.30 p.m. on Monday 9 July 1877 with play taking place at the club's then home beside the London & South Western Railway in Worple Road, Wimbledon. Twenty-two men each paid a guinea to take part with one, an old Etonian by the name of C.F. Buller, dropping out before a ball had even been hit. The final saw local land surveyor Spencer Gore comfortably defeat William Marshall 6–1, 6–2, 6–4 in just 48 minutes, the match having been postponed several times over a number of days due to a combination of bad weather plus the annual Eton versus Harrow cricket match – a highlight of the social season – taking place at Lords. As for the Women's final? Well there wasn't one. Not until 1884 did the ladies get a competition all to themselves with 19-year-old Maud Watson beating her elder sister Lilian 6–8, 6–3, 6–3 in the final.

THE SWITCH

Well before the outbreak of the First World War it had become blindingly obvious that the 8,000 ground capacity at Worple Road was inadequate. And so the All England Club, to coin its abbreviated title, started looking around for a new site. It eventually settled on an area of land off Church Road to the north of Wimbledon town centre, moving to its new home in 1922. At the time the relocation was seen as something of a gamble, costing as it did approximately £140,000. The club has stayed put ever since. In fact there's probably more chance of hell freezing over than Wimbledon moving from Church Road.

IT'S FUN TO STAY AT THE . . .

Back in the day, players came from all over Britain to take part in the Wimbledon Championships. Now they come from all corners of the world. The richer ones stay in plush houses within spitting distance of Church Road, usually rented out during Wimbledon fortnight by the owners. Those with smaller bank balances have to make do with hostels, budget hotels, the settee at a mate's house – anywhere basically with a roof and running water. Take Peter Doohan for example. In 1987 the little-known Australian dumped Boris Becker, winner of the

1985 and 1986 Men's Singles finals, out of Wimbledon in the second round. At the time he was staying at the YMCA hostel a few miles down the road in Surbiton, handing over £11 per night for the privilege. Incidentally, it was this defeat and the media hype which surrounded it that drew the following memorable response from Becker:

'Of course I am disappointed but I didn't lose a war. There is no one dead. It was just a tennis match.'

THE ICE MAN COMETH

Of the thousands of players to grace the All England Club's grass down the years few have matched the achievements of Björn Borg, dubbed the 'ice man' or 'ice Borg' for his calm on-court demeanour even when things threatened to go against him – which, to be fair, they rarely did. Borg helped make tennis sexy during the 1970s and in the process drove a coach and horses through the stuffy corridors of power at Wimbledon. At the end of his match against Roger Taylor in 1973 schoolgirls even stampeded onto the hallowed Centre Court turf to mob their idol before being escorted away by police. Sporting a trademark headband, the Swede won his first Wimbledon Singles final in 1976 going on to repeat the feat in 1977, 1978, 1979 and 1980. In the process he made history by winning 41 consecutive matches at the All England Club, John McEnroe finally throwing a spanner in the works come the 1981 final in what was destined to be Borg's last appearance at Wimbledon. Failed marriages, business ventures and comebacks followed together with rumours of an attempted suicide but nothing can erase the memory of Borg at his peak, collapsing to his knees in jubilation after yet another Championship win.

THE SWEDISH INVASION

Björn Borg's success inspired a whole new generation of Swedes to take up tennis during the 1970s and early '80s. Unquestionably the most successful when it came to Wimbledon was Stefan Edberg who reached three Singles finals, winning two of them (both against Boris Becker in 1988 and 1990). He would have reached the final in 1991 as well had it not been for the German Michael Stich. Incredibly, Edberg won all his service games in their semi-final encounter yet still ended up losing the match, Stich dominating in the tie breaks 4–6, 7–6, 7–6, 7–6.

THE AUSSIE INVASION

A trickle. That's what the Swedish invasion amounted to when compared with the Australian deluge that flooded Wimbledon during the 1950s, '60s and early '70s. Of the sixteen Championships spanning the years 1956 to 1971, six different Australians won the Men's Singles event a total of 13 times (more often than not beating one of their compatriots in the final). Three of those titles went to John Newcombe, owner of possibly the finest moustache ever to grace a tennis court. And yet not even Newcombe could hold a candle to the man reckoned to be the finest

Australian player of them all – Rod Laver. Shy of nature and wiry of build, the diminutive 'Rocket' (he stood just 5ft 8in and came from Rockingham, Queensland) won Wimbledon in 1961, 1962, 1968 and 1969 on his way to becoming the game's first millionaire. There would almost certainly have been more titles had he not turned professional in 1963 (Wimbledon remained an amateurs-only event until 1967, going pro the following year). Australia's domination of the era wasn't entirely down to the men either. Margaret Smith won the Ladies' Singles title in 1963, 1965 and 1970 (the latter under her married name of Margaret Court) while Yvonne Goolagong, later to become Yvonne Cawley, was crowned queen of the Centre Court in both 1971 and 1980.

UNLUCKY FOUR

One of the finest Australian exports was Ken Rosewall, a man who racked up 32 titles around the world in a memorable career lasting the best part of 30 years. He won the lot – the US Open, Roland Garros, the Australian Open – all of them except for Wimbledon, though not through lack of trying. Rosewall reached the Men's Singles final on four occasions and lost every time, his last shot at glory in 1974 (aged 39) ending in a humiliating straight sets defeat to the hip new gunslinger in town, Jimmy Connors. Two months later he got the chance to wreak his revenge on Connors in the final of the US Open. To the disappointment of tennis romantics the world over Rosewall lost again in what proved to be his swansong in a Grand Slam final.

GORAN THE GREAT

Like Ken Rosewall, so Goran Ivanisevic seemed destined never to win Wimbledon. In 1992 the Croatian maverick lost an epic final to Andre Agassi while in 1994 and 1998 he finished runner-up on both occasions to 'Pistol' Pete Sampras. By 2001 his career was seriously on the wane. The previous November Ivanisevic had been forced to retire halfway through a match in Brighton having smashed all his racquets in frustration at his poor form. He only made it into the Wimbledon Men's Singles draw because the All England Club gave him a wildcard in recognition of his previous good form at the Championships. What happened next remains little short of a sporting miracle. Fuelled on painkillers to keep his injury-ravaged body in check, the player ranked 126 in the world somehow managed to turn back the clock and make it through to the final, breaking British hearts along the way by defeating Greg Rusedski in the fourth round plus Tim Henman in a rain-delayed semi which took three days to complete. The dire weather meant his showdown against the popular Australian Pat Rafter was held over to a third Monday with tickets for the match going on sale that morning. As a consequence the Centre Court atmosphere resembled that of a football match as thousands of Croats and Aussies (plus a few Brits) cheered themselves hoarse for over 3 hours, Ivanisevic eventually prevailing 9–7 in the fifth set to become the only wildcard to date ever to win the Men's final. Over the course of the 2001 Championships he served an incredible 212 aces spanning seven matches, beating his own previous record of 206 set in 1992.

THE CLIMB

They all do it now, even Goran Ivanisevic. No sooner has the final point of the final match been played than the victor is on his or her way up to the Centre Court players' box to embrace friends and loved ones. But who started it all? That honour falls to Pat Cash who made the inaugural climb in 1987 after seeing off Ivan Lendl to win the only Grand Slam title of his career. Rafael Nadal went one further following his 2008 Men's final win over Roger Federer, creeping gingerly across the top of broadcasting booths to greet Prince Felipe and Princess Letizia of Spain in the Royal Box.

LOOK OUT – CLIFF!

Some remember it as an act of gay spontaneity the like of which Britain will probably never see again. Others would rather forget about it altogether. On 3 July 1996 during a prolonged break in play due to rain, the singer Cliff Richard – himself a keen tennis fan and member of the All England Club – took hold of a microphone while standing in the Centre Court Royal Box and serenaded the waiting crowd (not to mention a live TV audience of millions) with songs from his back catalogue including *Summer Holiday* and *Living Doll*. To make matters better/worse, depending on your standpoint, he was joined on backing vocals by various female tennis players including Virginia Wade and Pam Shriver. Richard has since maintained that he was put in an impossible situation by being asked to sing having merely agreed to do an interview for radio. Still, it worked in his favour. As a consequence of Richard's impromptu performance advance ticket sales for his show *Heathcliff*, based loosely on the novel *Wuthering Heights* by Emily Brontë, showed a healthy increase.

THE CRYING GAME

Goran Ivanisevic filled up during the closing stages of his 2001 Men's final victory over Pat Rafter. Many were seen dissolving during Cliff Richard's Centre Court sing-a-long, albeit for wildly contrasting reasons. As long as there is a Wimbledon Championships, there will be tears. Rarely a day goes by during the fortnight without someone breaking down, though it usually tends to happen off-court away from the public's gaze (yours truly has been forced to curtail several post match interviews with weepy-eyed players in no fit state to talk). Perhaps the most famous cry of them all occurred in 1993 at the end of the Women's Singles final between Steffi Graf and Jana Novotna. The latter had been within a point of taking a 5–1 lead in the third and final set when she suddenly suffered an attack of the nerves. Or, to use the sporting term, she began to 'choke'. Graf went on to win the next five games and take the title. During the subsequent presentation ceremony the unfortunate Novotna burst into tears and cried on the Duchess of Kent's shoulder, the royal doing her best under the circumstances by saying she was sure her day would eventually come. Five years later it did when Novotna beat Nathalie Tauziat of France to become Wimbledon Champion.

BAGELS

The main reason why most players go into emotional meltdown following a match at Wimbledon is because they've been beaten. For the ladies the worst losing margin you can get is 6–0, 6–0, whereas for the gents (who play the best of five sets) it's 6–0, 6–0, 6–0. Those big fat zeros make the bagel reference self-explanatory. There have been plenty of 6–0, 6–0 scorelines in the Women's Singles event. In fact most years some unfortunate female will fail to win a solitary game. Marlene Weingartner of Germany took things to extremes in 1999, losing her second-round Singles match 6–0, 6–0 before exiting the Women's Doubles competition in the first round by exactly the same score. However, in the men's game bagels are far rarer. Stefan Edberg managed to beat fellow Swede Stefan Eriksson 6–0, 6–0, 6–0 in 1987 but that was the first whitewash in the Men's Singles at Wimbledon since 1947. At the time of writing no one has since managed to repeat Edberg's feat.

THE HAND IN HAND

Those players failing to win a single game could do worse than drown their sorrows at the Hand in Hand pub, a favourite watering hole of tennis aficionados situated a good walk from Church Road near the south-west corner of Wimbledon Common. Throughout the years many a spectator, sports writer and player has retreated here at the end of a long day to unwind. In 2009 the popular American Doubles pair Bob and Mike Bryan even played a gig at the Hand in Hand with their group, the Bryan Brothers Band. For the record drummer Mike is two minutes older than his twin Bob who plays the keyboard.

THE SOUND OF THE SUBURBS

Every year a sizeable number of Wimbledon competitors use music as a way of psyching themselves up before going into battle, listening to favourite songs while killing time in the changing rooms. Take Andy Murray for example. In 2005 the Scotsman turned to the Black Eyed Peas for inspiration in what was his first Grand Slam tournament since graduating from the junior ranks. And to a point it worked, Murray progressing to the third round where he lost a nail-biting five-setter to David Nalbandian. Four years earlier another Brit, a Lancastrian by the name of Barry Cowan, took headphones onto Court 1 with him for a second-round match against Pete Sampras. During breaks in play Cowan – a devoted fan of Liverpool Football Club – listened repeatedly to the club's anthem 'You'll Never Walk Alone' by Gerry and the Pacemakers as he almost pulled off one of the biggest Wimbledon shocks of all time, fighting back from two sets down against the all-conquering Sampras before eventually losing 3–6, 2–6, 7–6, 6–4, 3–6. Afterwards it was declared that the wearing of headphones during rest breaks in a match would no longer be allowed, just in case the player's coach was passing on instructions. The killjoys.

AN UNLIKELY AMATEUR

Chrissie Hynde, lead singer with The Pretenders, was inspired to write her hit song 'Don't Get Me Wrong' by watching John McEnroe in action. Today the popular New Yorker earns a handsome crust as Wimbledon's number one television pundit, dividing his time between working for the BBC and NBC of America. However, it was a different story altogether back in 1977 when he first came to Wimbledon as a complete unknown. Despite still being an amateur, the brash 18-year-old made it all the way to the semi-finals where he lost to Jimmy Connors. McEnroe's financial reward for doing so? Absolutely nothing. As an amateur he wasn't allowed to be paid. McEnroe eventually turned professional in June 1978 and more than made up for the hole in his wallet by winning Wimbledon in 1981, 1983 and 1984.

PRIZE MONEY

Up until 1968 when tennis finally went professional nobody 'officially' earned a penny for competing at Wimbledon (the payment of backhanders to amateurs was however rife throughout the sport, hence the term 'shamateurism' frequently being used). In fact during the early years of the tournament players ended up out of pocket having had to pay an initial entrance fee for the honour of competing. When Rod Laver won the Men's final in 1968 he was rewarded with a cheque for £2,000 which nowadays wouldn't come close to paying for one of Roger Federer's extravagant cream suits (for the record Federer bagged a cool £850,000 for winning Wimbledon in 2009). And if you think that's paltry then pity Billie Jean King, winner of the Women's Singles in 1968, who collected just £750 in prize money for her efforts. Which brings us neatly on to. . . .

EQUAL PAY

For 29 years the winner of the Wimbledon Men's Singles final went home with more prize money than the Women's Singles Champion. In 1978 Björn Borg banked £19,000 compared to Martina Navratilova who had to make do with £17,100. Steffi Graf took home £148,500 in 1988, a tidy sum but still £16,500 down on Stefan Edberg's haul. By the end of the twentieth century the issue of equal pay at Wimbledon had become a real hot potato with Billie Jean King, one of the loudest voices in the women's corner. 'Hang on a minute,' said more than a few men. 'We play the best of five sets, you play the best of three. Some of your matches are finished inside 60 minutes whereas ours can go on for 4 or 5 hours. Why should you earn the same as us?' In the end the principle of equal pay triumphed, 2007 proving to be the watershed year of parity. Now a third-round loser in the Women's Singles will earn exactly the same as a third-round loser in the Men's competition, something that also applies in the Doubles events. Wimbledon was the last of the Grand Slam tennis events to bow to the equal pay lobby.

PRETTY GREEN

Wimbledon may have joined the twenty-first century when it comes to equal pay but there remains one area where it has steadfastly refused to bend. Tennis was meant to be played on grass – the sport was initially called 'lawn tennis' after all. Not that the French would agree. At Roland Garros they persist on using filthy old clay while hard courts remain the surface of choice for the US Open. The Australian Open was played on grass until 1988 when they thought better of it and decided to go with the hard stuff, leaving Wimbledon all on its own. And that's the way it's likely to stay – at least until global warming turns SW19 into a desert.

SW19

What is 'SW19' and why do sports writers and BBC commentators always bang on about it during Wimbledon fortnight? SW19 is in fact the London postal area in which the Championships take place and should not be confused with any kind of incapacity benefit form that might go by a similar sounding name. The official postcode in full, for you sat-nav lovers, is SW19 5AE.

THE SAINT

The third man ever to win the Wimbledon Men's Singles title was a North Yorkshireman by the name of John Hartley, otherwise known to his parishioners in rural

Burneston as the Reverend John Thorneycroft Hartley. This man of the cloth hadn't expected to reach the latter stages of Wimbledon which explains his return home on the middle Saturday of the 1879 tournament to fulfil religious duties the following day. Come Monday afternoon he was back at Worple Road ready for his semi-final having caught a train from Thirsk to King's Cross station that morning before hot-footing it across London to the All England Club. He duly won, despite the haphazard pre-match preparation, going on to defeat the Irishman Vere Thomas St Leger Goold in the final. Hartley successfully defended his title in 1880 and reached the final again in 1881 only to be absolutely crucified – not literally of course – by William Renshaw in a match that lasted just 37 minutes, the shortest recorded time for a Men's Singles final at Wimbledon.

THE SINNER

Several years after losing to John Hartley in the 1879 final, Vere Thomas St Leger Goold was found guilty along with his wife Marie Girodin of killing a wealthy Danish widow by the name of Emma Liven in Monte Carlo. He was sentenced to penal servitude for life on Devil's Island, French Guiana, where he died in 1909 at the age of 54 by which time Hartley had become an Honorary Canon of Ripon Cathedral. Now there's a salutary lesson in right and wrong for you.

ROGER AND OUT – OR IN?

Like John Hartley, Roger Taylor was a proud Yorkshireman – albeit one from the more industrial southern end of the county (Sheffield) as opposed to the picturesque, rolling Dales. In the 1973 quarter-finals Taylor was paired against the 17-year-old Björn Borg, playing his first Wimbledon. At match point to Taylor in the fifth set, Borg suffered a 'dodgy' line call against him. Taylor was through to the semis – or was he? In a remarkable act of sportsmanship the dark-haired left-hander from the Steel City insisted on replaying the point. Ultimately it didn't cost him and Taylor eventually triumphed 6–1, 6–8, 3–6, 6–3, 7–5, his position as a player of principle and integrity firmly established.

DISQUALIFIED

Not all visitors to the All England Club are as impeccably behaved as Roger Taylor. That in mind, here's a question for you. Who was the first player ever to be disqualified from Wimbledon? Was it:

a.) John McEnroe
b.) Jimmy Connors
c.) Ilie Nastase
d.) Tim Henman

Need some help? Okay then, here's a clue. It wasn't McEnroe. Or Connors. That means it must have been the tantrum prone Nastase, right? Well, er, no. Incredible as it sounds the first man to be disqualified from Wimbledon was Tim 'whiter-than-white' Henman. The day of shame was Wednesday 28 June 1995, the place Court 14. Henman was partnering fellow Brit Jeremy Bates against the American Jeff Tarango and Henrik Holm of Sweden. Henman and Bates were leading 2–1 in sets with the score delicately poised at 6–6 in the fourth when the former made a mistake to lose a point. Picking up a loose ball, Henman proceeded to fire it down the court in frustration. Poor Caroline Hall, a 16-year-old ball girl, never stood a chance. It struck her in the head sending the teenager tumbling to the turf amid tears of pain and, no doubt, embarrassment. Umpire Wayne McEwan was left with no other option but to disqualify Henman, causing the British pair to default the match. Give Henman credit though; he issued a public apology and found enough spare cash to buy Hall flowers despite being £1,910 out of pocket due to the subsequent fine. Why do so few people remember this incident? A couple of reasons. One, it happened before Henman found fame and was therefore less newsworthy. And two, because of what occurred three days later at Wimbledon across on Court 13.

TARANGO'S MELTDOWN

Jeff Tarango, one half of Henman's opposing Doubles team that fateful day, had a reputation for losing his temper big time. A middling tennis professional, he was the kind of player good enough to qualify automatically for the Wimbledon Singles draw but without a cat's chance in hell of making the latter stages (partly, as some felt, because he was unable to keep his emotions in check). In 1995 the 26-year-old had made it further than ever before at SW19, reaching the third round and a date with Alexander Mronz of Germany. Tarango lost the first set 6–7, then had a serve called out which he believed to have been an ace. Words were exchanged between the fiery Californian and umpire Bruno Rebeuh of France, prompting slow handclaps and jeers from the crowd. Tarango told them to shut up and was given a warning. 'How come they can say whatever they want to me?' he roared. 'Can you call the supervisor please, I have a big beef.' Along came the supervisor who upheld the warning. At which point Tarango turned on Rebeuh. 'You are the most corrupt official in the game and you can't do that.' Rebeuh then called a point penalty against Tarango who threw down two balls in his possession before loudly declaring, 'No way. That's it.' And off he stropped. Shortly afterwards, Tarango's French wife Benedicte heaped more fuel on the fire by slapping Rebeuh in the face as the official made his way back to the umpire's office. This time, unlike the Henman incident, there was no apology. So Tarango became the first man to be disqualified from the Singles at Wimbledon, receiving a fine and ban from the following year's Championships. 'I was seeing red,' he has since said of the matter. 'I thought something really bad was going to happen if I did not leave the court. People say I was thrown out of Wimbledon but in fact I chose to leave.'

WOOD'S WALK-OVER

Jeff Tarango's 1995 visit to Wimbledon may have ended in ignominy but at least he made it on court to play his match. In 1931 the American Frank Shields, grandfather to the actress Brooke Shields, picked up a slight ankle injury during his semi-final Men's Singles win over the legendary French player Jean Borotra. With the Americans due to take on Britain in an important Davis Cup tie immediately after Wimbledon, the USA team captain Gene Dixon took the extraordinary precaution of withdrawing Shields from the final due to the supposedly dodgy state of the ankle. As a result Sidney Wood, also a member of the American Davis Cup squad, became Wimbledon Champion without even hitting a ball by way of a walk-over. In farcical circumstances the final was cancelled to the immense disappointment of the tennis world and those lucky enough to have tickets for the match. However, justice was seen to be done when the Americans – by now fully rested thanks to the cancellation of the final and with Shields showing no signs of any 'injury' – went down 3–2 to Britain in the Davis Cup, Shields losing the deciding rubber to Henry 'Bunny' Austin.

FACE-OFF

So tennis is meant to be a nice social game with little risk of serious injury, right? Tell that to poor Ethel Larcombe. In 1913 while competing in a Mixed Doubles tie, Larcombe was hit in the face with such force by a ball that she had to retire not just from the match but also the Women's Singles event which she had won the previous year. The black-and-blue Larcombe was by all accounts inconsolable having already reached the final of the Singles, her withdrawal handing the title to Dorothea Lambert-Chambers by way of a walk-over. To make matters worse for the Wimbledon authorities Charlotte Sterry then suffered a leg injury leaving her unable to compete in the final of the Women's Doubles, resulting in yet another walk-over. Not exactly a vintage Championships, 1913.

BACK TO REALITY

At least Tommy Ho's injury, suffered while partnering Brett Steven in the 1995 Men's Doubles competition, assured him of a place in the record books – albeit an unwanted one. During the very first point of their second-round tie against Cristian Brandi and Marcos Ondruska, Ho injured his back while attempting to intercept a return. Wimbledon's shortest ever match had come to its conclusion, Ho retiring with the score at 0–0, 0–15. Unfortunately the back failed to heal properly leading to his premature retirement from the sport two years later.

DERNOVSKYY OFF-SKY

Peter-Jon Nomdo of South Africa was another player for whom a trip to Wimbledon ended in injury, though not the kind anyone could have predicted. Nomdo, a competitor in the Boys' Doubles event at the 2000

Championships, was on the receiving end of an assault by fellow junior Andriy Dernovskyy which took place in the players' halls of residence at nearby Roehampton Institute. The incident left the Wimbledon authorities with no option but to disqualify Dernovskyy, the second time within the space of 12 months that such recourse had been used against a junior player. In 1999 David Nalbandian arrived late for his Boys' Singles semi-final match prompting the young Argentinian's disqualification from the Championships.

ONE OF A KIND

In 1947 Hans Redl of Austria progressed to the fourth round of the Men's Singles event at Wimbledon. Nothing of particular significance about that you might think. Not until I tell you that Redl had lost his left arm while on active service during the Second World War, fighting at the Battle of Stalingrad. As a result special dispensation was granted for him to touch the ball twice every time he served, tossing the ball into the air with his racquet before hitting it. Redl went on to compete at Wimbledon until 1956.

IN THE WARS

The arrival of the First World War saw the Championships suspended from 1915 until 1919, during which the All England Club managed to survive on donations from members and wealthy benefactors. By the time hostilities resumed again in 1939 Wimbledon had moved across town from Worple Road to Church Road becoming a larger, more resilient and far less amateur operation in the process. Between 1940 and 1945 the club remained open to members though the Championships themselves were suspended, the grounds being used for a variety of war-related purposes including civil defence training. On the night of 11 October 1940 a 'stick' of 500lb bombs caused considerable damage to the club's grounds with one striking the Centre Court roof. This meant the crowd capacity of Wimbledon's most famous arena was reduced for the first three Championships after the war while rebuilding work took place.

DAN THE MAN

Dan Maskell, a former professional tennis player and coach to the British Davis Cup squad during the 1930s glory years of Fred Perry and Henry 'Bunny' Austin, received an OBE for his services as an RAF rehabilitation officer helping injured airmen return to the skies during the Second World War. However, Dan is best remembered today not for his playing, coaching or rehabilitation skills. To millions he will always be the 'Voice of Wimbledon' for his work as a television commentator, a job he fulfilled from 1952 right up until the year before his death in 1992. Dan belonged to the 'less is more' school of commentary. Sometimes he wouldn't say anything for two or three points, sparking fears that he'd popped off for a swift half or gone to meet his maker. Yet Dan knew his stuff. If he didn't say anything, that's probably because there wasn't anything to say. He let the pictures speak for themselves, his 'Oh I say!' catchphrase telling viewers all they needed to know about a standout moment. John McEnroe may have the sound bites today but there has never been anyone else quite like Dan.

DAN-ISMS

Dan Maskell commentated on Wimbledon for 39 years so we can forgive him the occasional gaffe. Try some of these Dan-isms for size:

'Lendl has remained throughout as calm as the proverbial iceberg.'

'The Gullikson twins here. An interesting pair, both from Wisconsin.'

'There is Peter Graf, Steffi's father, with his head on his chin.'

'You can almost hear the silence as they battle it out.'

'And here's Zivojinovic, six foot six inches tall and fourteen pounds ten ounces.'

'When Martina is tense it helps her relax.'

SUE'S NEAR MISS

One of Dan Maskell's more memorable commentaries came in 1977 when he guided viewers through Virginia Wade's victory over Holland's Betty Stöve in the final of the Women's Singles event ('She's done it!'). What hardly anyone remembers today – with the possible exception of former player turned BBC sports presenter Sue Barker – is that Wimbledon came within a whisker that year of having two British women competing against each other in the final. Wade booked her place in the last two with a three sets win over Chris Evert. The other semi-final also went to three sets, Stöve defeating Devon's very own Miss Barker, then just 21 years old, by 6–4, 2–6, 6–4. It was the closest Barker ever came to a Wimbledon final, the one Grand Slam title of her career having arrived the previous year at Roland Garros. What Britain would give for two Singles semi-finalists in the same year now!

QUEEN OF THE CENTRE COURT

Despite being patron of the All England Club, Her Majesty Queen Elizabeth II doesn't really 'do' Wimbledon. The last of her three trips to SW19 came on 1 July 1977 when she sat through Virginia Wade's Singles triumph over Betty Stöve, presenting 'Ginny' with the trophy afterwards. Her two previous visits came in 1957 and 1962 when she presented the winning trophies to Althea Gibson (the first black player ever to win Wimbledon) and Rod Laver respectively.

BY GEORGE!

With an attendance record that can best be described as 'wonky', we can only presume Queen Elizabeth II didn't inherit her father's love of tennis. Way back in 1926 when he was still known as the Duke of York, King George VI played at Wimbledon in the Men's Doubles competition partnering Louis Greig (later to become Sir Louis Greig, chairman of the All England Club). The duo were, however, soundly beaten in the first round by the veteran pairing of Herbert Roper Barrett and Arthur Gore, the latter a former three-time Wimbledon Men's Singles Champion.

STEFFI'S ROYAL FLUSH

It used to be the case that all players upon entering and leaving Wimbledon's Centre Court had to bow or curtsey in the direction of the Royal Box. Failure to do so automatically resulted in a one-way trip to the Tower of London. Oh alright, I've just made that up, but it was certainly frowned upon as Steffi Graf can testify. On her Wimbledon debut in 1984 Graf made it through to the fourth round of the Singles where she lost a tight three-set match on Centre Court to Britain's Jo Durie. Afterwards Graf, clearly peeved at the outcome, steamed off in the direction of the showers without so much as a glance in the direction of the Royal Box, drawing boos from the crowd and a general shake of the head from Fleet Street's finest. In 2003 the Duke of Kent, in his role as the All England Club's president, decided to modify this somewhat outdated if quaintly British tradition, requesting that players should only bow or curtsey to the Royal Box when either the Queen or the Prince of Wales are present.

GRASS IS GREAT . . . IF YOU ARE A COW

Andre Agassi, Steffi Graf's future husband, was initially ambivalent to say the least about Wimbledon. After losing to the flamboyant Frenchman Henri Leconte in the first round of the 1987 tournament, Agassi skipped the next three Championships amid murmurs that he didn't care much for grass, strawberries, the shabby state of the departure lounge at Heathrow . . . you get the picture. He returned in 1991 to reach the quarter-finals before winning Wimbledon the following year, after which Agassi suddenly decided that he adored the place. All of which goes to show that those players who slag Wimbledon off tend not to have very good records there. Coincidence? You decide for yourself. With the exception of Jimmy Connors, the following quotes came from players whose Wimbledon records were, how shall I put it, less than perfect:

'Wimbledon is the world's most boring tournament. There's hardly anything to do apart from tennis. You constantly find yourself yawning – there's no entertainment here.'

Nikolay Davydenko

'Grass is great if you are a cow, but not so great if you are a tennis player.'

Manuel Orantes

'New Yorkers love it when you spill your guts out there. Spill your guts at Wimbledon and they make you stop and clean it up.'

Jimmy Connors

'I don't take Wimbledon, like playing on grass, like a really important thing. Tennis, when you see it on grass, it's not tennis. It's not a surface to watch or play tennis on. It's really boring.'

Marcelo Rios

'We get £20 for lunch. I have a coach and a masseuse and one portion of the most uneatable spaghetti costs £12, a portion of tasteless strawberries costs £5, coffee another £5. The rest of the food is horrible, fish and chips everywhere and hamburgers.'

Marat Safin

BOUNDING BASQUE

While Marat Safin was 'relieved, pretty much relieved' to play his last match at Wimbledon in 2009 before retiring, only the hands of time prevented Jean Borotra from rolling up at SW19 every year, racquets at the ready. The charismatic 'Bounding Basque' first played at Wimbledon in 1922, his final appearance at the Championships coming in 1976 when he competed in the Veterans'

Doubles event aged 77. In between he was crowned Men's Singles Champion in 1924 and 1926, concentrating solely on the Doubles competitions from the early 1930s onwards. He died in Arbonne, France, in 1994, three weeks short of what would have been his 96th birthday.

GROUNDHOG DAY

Ann Jones could have been forgiven for absolutely despising Wimbledon. On five occasions (1958, 1960, 1962, 1963 and 1966) the left-hander from Birmingham went out at the semi-final stage of the Women's Singles, enough to shatter any player's self-belief. In 1967, at long last, Jones made the final where she lost to Billie Jean King, only to suffer more semi-final heartache the following year. By 1969 Britain could barely watch as Jones again reached the last four. She lost a titanic first set to Margaret Court by 10–12 (tie-breaks had yet to be introduced) but came storming back to win the next two and stake her place in the final where, to the joy of an entire nation, Jones defeated King to become Wimbledon Champion.

WONDER WOMAN

Unlike Ann Jones, Martina Navratilova made winning Wimbledon look easy to the point where it almost became dull. Only now she has finally retired can we fully appreciate the extent of her remarkable achievements. Here is Martina's incredible SW19 Singles record spanning 1978 to 1990 in full:

1978: Champion (beat Chris Evert 2–6, 6–4, 7–5)
1979: Champion (beat Mrs J.M. Lloyd 6–4, 6–4)
1980: Semi-Finalist (lost to Mrs J.M. Lloyd 6–4, 4–6, 2–6)
1981: Semi-Finalist (lost to Hana Mandlikova 5–7, 6–4, 1–6)
1982: Champion (beat Mrs J.M. Lloyd 6–1, 3–6, 6–2)
1983: Champion (beat Andrea Jaeger 6–0, 6–3)
1984: Champion (beat Mrs J.M. Lloyd 7–6, 6–2)
1985: Champion (beat Mrs J.M. Lloyd 4–6, 6–3, 6–2)
1986: Champion (beat Hana Mandlikova 7–6, 6–3)
1987: Champion (beat Steffi Graf 7–5, 6–3)
1988: Runner-up (lost to Steffi Graf 7–5, 2–6, 1–6)
1989: Runner-up (lost to Steffi Graf 2–6, 7–6, 1–6)
1990: Champion (beat Zina Garrison 6–4, 6–1)

Not bad, eh? On top of that Martina made the final in 1994 (losing to Conchita Martinez), the semi-finals in 1976, 1992 and 1993 plus the quarter-finals in 1975, 1977 and 1991. She also won the Women's Doubles event seven times and the Mixed Doubles competition on four occasions. In 2004, aged 47, she once again played in the Singles at Wimbledon, thrashing Catalina Castaño of Colombia 6–0, 6–1 in the first round. No wonder Martina is many people's choice as the outstanding female tennis player of all time.

SISTER ACT

Several years after losing to Martina Navratilova in the 1983 Women's final Andrea Jaeger, later to become a Dominican nun (really!), made an extraordinary confession.

The night before the final Jaeger had a blazing row with her father which culminated in the 18-year-old seeking refuge at a nearby flat rented by, you've guessed it, Martina Navratilova. Being the kind soul that she is, Martina took her in despite the catastrophic effect such a charitable gesture might have on her own pre-match preparation. Feeling embarrassed about what had happened, Jaeger now says she deliberately didn't try in the final in order to 'make it right' with her opponent. Whatever the truth of the matter, Jaeger certainly wasn't at the races against a player she had beaten the previous week at Eastbourne, sliding to a 6–0, 6–3 defeat in just 54 minutes.

JIMMY'S NEMESIS

Like Martina Navratilova, Jimmy Connors tended to crush most of those put in front of him at Wimbledon. During the course of his illustrious career, the brash American from Belleville, Illinois, won 84 Singles matches at the All England Club, more than Andre Agassi (46), Boris Becker (71), Björn Borg (51), Stefan Edberg (49), Rod Laver (50), Ivan Lendl (48), John McEnroe (59) or even Pete Sampras (63). However, when it came to head-to-head clashes at Wimbledon, Borg seemed to have something of a hex over Connors. They first met in the 1977 Men's final, Borg winning a tight five-set match that lasted over 3 hours. The following year Borg again defeated Connors in the final, this time in straight sets. Twelve months later they met in the semi-finals, Borg administering another straight sets spanking on his way to a fourth consecutive Wimbledon title.

Denied an opportunity to exact some revenge in 1980, Connors went hell for leather at Borg in their 1981 semi-final winning the opening two sets 6–0, 6–4. And then it all went horribly wrong for 'Jimbo'. Cool as ever, Borg fought back to comfortably win the next three sets for the loss of just seven games. Why does the Swede remember this victory with particular fondness? Because it was the last match he ever won at Wimbledon, John McEnroe finally breaking the Swede's stranglehold on the Men's Singles competition in the final.

END OF AN ERA

In 1974 Jimmy Connors won Wimbledon with a metal-framed Wilson T-2000, unwittingly changing racquet technology (and some might say the entire sport of tennis) forever. By 1988 the transformation was complete. For the first time no player used a wooden racquet while competing at the Championships.

McENROE'S PERFECT MATCH

Not even his trusty Wilson T-2000 could save Jimmy Connors from utter humiliation against John McEnroe in the Men's Singles final of 1984. In what was expected to be a close contest, McEnroe played what many still regard as the closest thing to the perfect tennis match, making just three unforced errors on his way to a 6–1, 6–1, 6–2 victory.

WATTS THE SCORE?

They say there are no easy points to be had when it comes to Grand Slam tennis. However, umpire Ted Watts made a mockery of this common assumption at Wimbledon in 2004 while chairing a second-round Women's Singles match between Karolina Sprem and Venus Williams. Sprem was leading 2–1 in a second set tie-break when she won a point to go 3–1 ahead, only for Watts to announce the score as 4–1. Neither player realised the mistake and so no protest was made. Sprem kept her nerve to see out the tie-break 8–6, winning the match 7–6, 7–6. 'I don't think one call makes a match,' said a diplomatic Williams afterwards, sparing the unfortunate Watts any further embarrassment.

TWIN CHAMPIONS

Despite their remarkable talents, the Williams sisters have never exactly been firm favourites with the Wimbledon crowds. Dominance in sport can breed a strange kind of resentment (just ask Martina Navratilova) so perhaps the achievements of Venus and Serena will only be fully appreciated in years to come. William and Ernest Renshaw, however, had no such problems regarding their public image. Born in Leamington, Warwickshire, on 3 January 1861, the Renshaw twins did more than anyone to transform a pastime into a sport during Wimbledon's infancy. So popular did the pair become that the All England Club installed a railway platform beside the Worple Road grounds to cope with the crowds flooding in every year to watch them in action. William was the outstanding player of his era, winning Wimbledon seven times (1881–6 and 1889). Mind you, Ernest was certainly no slouch becoming Men's Singles Champion himself in 1888 and finishing runner-up three times, losing to his brother on each occasion.

SEVENTY-SEVEN . . .

. . . was the percentage of British spectators at the 2003 Wimbledon Championships unable to name a UK player competing other than Tim Henman or Greg Rusedski.

BOGDANOVIC

The weather. Too middle class. The set up within the Lawn Tennis Association. The players aren't physically tough enough. The players aren't mentally tough enough. The players don't train hard enough. The ridiculous costs that come with playing a relatively simple sport . . . and so on. For longer than anyone cares to remember the inquest into why Britain underachieves so spectacularly as a tennis-playing nation has been rumbling on. Since the dawn of the twenty-first century one man more than any other has come to epitomise the failings of the British tennis system. Step forward Alex Bogdanovic. Wrong as it might seem to highlight a single person's failings, here is Alex's dismal record at Wimbledon up to and including 2009:

2002: Lost in the first round to Nicolas Escude
      4–6, 6–4, 6–4, 6–4
2003: Lost in the first round to Sargis Sargasian
      6–1, 6–3, 6–2
2004: Lost in the first round to Roger Federer
      6–3, 6–3, 6–0
2005: Lost in the first round to Kevin Kim
      6–7, 6–1, 6–4, 6–2
2006: Lost in the first round to Rafael Nadal
      6–4, 7–6, 6–4
2007: Lost in the first round to Chris Guccione
      7–6, 6–4, 6–4
2008: Lost in the first round to Simone Bolelli
      7–6, 4–6, 6–3, 7–6
2009: Lost in the first round to Tomas Berdych
      6–3, 6–4, 6–4

That's eight straight first-round defeats for Alex who relied on wildcards to get into Wimbledon due to his low world ranking. Those reverses still managed to net him £75,825 in prize money, something that rankles in the extreme with his burgeoning band of critics. To be fair, Alex could have done with avoiding Roger Federer or Rafael Nadal at the first hurdle, but you'd have thought he might nick a result somewhere along the line against one of the others. As a journalist observed after Alex's 2009 crash-and-burn, 'A Bogdanovic first-round defeat has become as much a part of the summer season as Royal Ascot or Henley.'

WILDCARDS

It goes without saying that you've got to be good at tennis to play at Wimbledon (even Alex Bogdanovic has been known to win the occasional match outside SW19). Traditionally the top 100 or so men and women tend to qualify automatically for the Singles events. Those who fail to make the cut can always hope for a wildcard. These are awarded by Wimbledon's very own wildcard committee as a way of increasing British interest in the competition, though overseas players with good previous records at the Championships also have a chance of being allocated one. Because of their low world rankings it's extremely rare for a wildcard to make it any further than the third round of the Singles. Only one player, Goran Ivanisevic, has ever won Wimbledon as a wildcard.

ROEHAMPTON

The next best thing for those players who miss out on a wildcard is to go through the Wimbledon qualification process. This takes place at the Bank of England Sports Ground in Roehampton the week prior to Wimbledon fortnight as dozens of players with three-figure world rankings battle it out for the last few places in the main draw. It's a desperate yet enthralling spectacle about as far removed from the Centre Court as you can get, with matches played out in front of handfuls rather than thousands of spectators. And amazingly it's free to watch! That's right, there's no admission fee. So if you want to see some decent tennis for absolutely nowt, then you know where to go. In 2000 Vladimir Voltchkov of Belarus made the semi-finals of Wimbledon having gone through the qualifying process, equalling the feat of a young 18-year-old called John McEnroe who also progressed to the last four in 1977. I wonder whatever happened to him?

AND . . . ACTION!

With a world ranking of 119, British player Peter Colt would have relied on either a wildcard or the qualifying process in order to compete in the Men's Singles draw at the All England Club. Had he existed that is because Peter Colt was in fact the fictional star of *Wimbledon,* the 2004 film in which a struggling thirty-something player has one last shot at winning the mother of all tennis tournaments. Large chunks of the movie were filmed during the 2003 Championships with spectators in effect playing the roles of unpaid extras. The cheapskates. Although the All England Club tends to be notoriously strict over use (or rather misuse) of the Wimbledon brand, three other films have also been granted permission to shoot inside the club's grounds. In September 1967 scenes from *Nobody Runs Forever* starring Rod Taylor and Christopher Plummer were recorded at Wimbledon. Eleven years later the Centre Court got a walk-on part in *The Players* starring Ali McGraw with filming taking place just before the Women's final between Martina Navratilova and Chris Evert. The Centre Court also appeared in the 1980 Burt Reynolds/David Niven film *Rough Cut,* over 600 extras being employed for crowd scenes which were shot after the 1979 Championships had finished.

FRED

'It must be a comedy if a British player is winning at Wimbledon!'

Serena Williams on the film Wimbledon

Hold your horses Serena. Rubbish as Britain has tended to be at tennis over recent decades, there's no escaping the fact that Fred Perry remains one of Wimbledon's all-time greats having won the Men's Singles title in 1934, 1935 and 1936. So what if he later became an American citizen, even going so far as serving in the US Army during the Second World War? The man was born in Stockport, the son of a trade union father, and that makes him about as British as the Manchester rain. Perry's big break came at Wimbledon in 1930. Under the noses of the Lawn Tennis Association's selection committee which was about to chose a British team to tour the USA and South America, he beat the fourth seed Humberto de Morpurgo (an Italian baron and First World War flying ace – seriously, you couldn't make this stuff up) in the third round. Perry was selected for the American tour and never looked back, winning the US Open three times plus the Australian and French Opens once each to go alongside his hat-trick of Wimbledon triumphs. After retiring from tennis he founded one of the world's best-known leisurewear companies, Fred Perry Sportswear, earning respect for his work as a sports writer and broadcaster. He died in 1995 in Melbourne, Australia, at the age of 85. On the unveiling of a statue in his honour at Wimbledon eleven years previously, Perry had said, 'I can only compare that sort of tribute to the Football Association putting up a statue to Stanley Matthews at Wembley Stadium.'

GREG RAGE

Whereas Fred Perry traded in his British passport for American citizenship, the Canadian left-hander Greg Rusedski opted to cross the Atlantic in the opposite direction. Despite his mother having been born in the Yorkshire town of Dewsbury, Rusedski struggled to win the hearts of some British tennis fans who regarded him as a Canadian interloper – that is until his match against Andy Roddick at the 2003 Wimbledon Championships. Upset by the umpire's refusal to replay a point after a spectator had called out in the middle of a rally, Rusedski embarked on a tirade which included a very British six letter swear word beginning in 'w' and ending in 'er'. You know the one. The word was picked up by a BBC microphone and broadcast live on TV, something the BBC (and later Rusedski) apologised for. Though lambasted by some reporters from the more highbrow corners of the media, the 'w***er' rant ended up earning Rusedski a new army of fans. As one tabloid journalist put it, 'Now we know he is officially one of us.'

FIRE AND RAIN

Jo Anne Russell would have been forgiven for turning the air blue ahead of her third-round Singles clash with Pam Casale at Wimbledon in 1982. When the car she had arranged to pick her up from a London hotel failed to show, Russell set off on foot expecting to hail a taxi. When that came to nothing she succeeded in thumbing a lift from a complete stranger, only for the car to develop an electrical fault and catch fire. Growing more desperate by the minute, Russell then took the extreme step of lying down in the road until another motorist stopped and picked her up. She arrived at Wimbledon an hour and 40 minutes late convinced she had been disqualified. Only then did Russell notice it was raining. Her match had been delayed!

WET, WET, WET

The British obsession with the weather tends to go into overdrive during Wimbledon fortnight. No, it's not just you. Collectively we all know that come the first day of the Championships it will rain. And rain. And rain. At some point during the tournament it will brighten up so the colossal backlog of matches can be played, then it will start raining again. It seems a precedent was set at the maiden Championships at Church Road in 1922 when the outside courts, uncovered and therefore open to the elements, were turned into quagmires by the incessant rain which resulted in the tournament being extended to a third Wednesday. Arguably the wettest Wimbledon of them all came in 1991 when only 52 of approximately 240 scheduled matches were completed during the first four days. A combination of early starts, play on the middle Sunday (a day traditionally reserved for rest) and slightly better weather during the second week meant the Championships, much to everyone's amazement, finished on time.

THE PERFECT STORM

The opening week of the 1985 Wimbledon Championships was, true to form, dogged by rain. And yet the showers that continually interrupted play were a drop in the ocean compared to the storm that hit SW19 on the afternoon of the second Friday, 5 July. As spectators ran for whatever cover they could find one-and-a-half inches of rain, plus the odd thunderbolt or two, was dumped on Wimbledon in the space of just 20 minutes. Play eventually resumed by which time several thousand people, soaked to the skin, had already left for the comfort of home.

WEATHER WARNING

'Wimbledon weather is always the same. Either it's rainy with sunny intervals or sunny with rainy intervals.'
Former player Pat Dupre

'We haven't had any more rain since it stopped raining.'
Harry Carpenter, ex-BBC commentator

'What would I do to improve Wimbledon? How about moving it to the summer?'
Pat Cash, former Wimbledon Men's Singles Champion turned BBC summariser

'I'm sure you're all fed up with me talking by now, and I'm starting to get fed up myself.'
BBC TV presenter Sue Barker grows tired of filling time between the showers, Wimbledon 2007

'I was absolutely in awe of the way they managed to cover the court. It was on before I'd put my things in my bag.'

Andre Agassi admires the speed of the Centre Court cover operators

'I love Wimbledon. But why don't they stage it in the summer?'

Former player Vijay Amritraj – and not the first to have this thought

RAISING THE ROOF

In 2004 the impossible happened. After years of denials, the All England Club announced that a retractable roof complete with floodlights would be built to cover the Centre Court. Not only would this keep the rain out but it would also allow matches to be played to a conclusion rather than being halted due to bad light. Construction work began in July 2006 and continued throughout 2007 and 2008, the roof being ready for the 2009 Championships. As if by magic, the weather throughout the entire fortnight was perfect.

ROOF RUNDOWN

The retractable roof weighs 1,000 tonnes and covers 5,200 square metres.

It takes between 8 and 10 minutes to close.

A further 30–40 minutes are then needed for what is known as the 'air management system' inside the arena to achieve the right conditions for play.

The roof stands approximately 16 metres above the Centre Court surface and is in two sections which come together when closed.

The roof was given a trial run ahead of the 2009 Wimbledon Championships when a capacity crowd of 15,000 watched Tim Henman and Kim Clijsters play the husband and wife team of Andre Agassi and Steffi Graf in an exhibition doubles match.

The roof made its competitive debut on Monday 29 June 2009 during a Women's fourth-round Singles match between Amelie Mauresmo and Dinara Safina. The first match to be completed from start to finish under the roof occurred later the same day, Andy Murray defeating Switzerland's Stanislas Wawrinka under the lights in a fourth-round, five-set match that lasted until 10.38 p.m.

The All England Club refused to say how much the Centre Court roof cost, but the general consensus is that the bill came to something in the region of £70–80 million.

MARATHON FINAL NUMBER ONE

Had the Centre Court roof been operational in 2008 then it would almost certainly have been used during the latter stages of the Men's Singles final between Roger Federer and Rafael Nadal. The five-set match – won by Nadal and regarded by many as the finest ever seen at SW19 – finished in virtual darkness after 4 hours 48 minutes, making it the longest Singles final in Wimbledon history in terms of time played.

MARATHON FINAL NUMBER TWO

The longest Wimbledon Singles final in terms of games played was the 2009 showdown between Roger Federer and Andy Roddick. There were 77 in all, Federer eventually triumphing 5–7, 7–6, 7–6, 3–6, 16–14 after 4 hours and 16 minutes to earn his fifteenth Grand Slam title. Federer served 50 aces on his way to victory, just one short of the all-time Wimbledon record. That belongs to Ivo Karlovic of Croatia who hit 51 in his 2005 first-round Men's Singles match against the Italian Daniele Bracciali.

NET GAIN

Following his marathon 2009 Men's Singles victory over Andy Roddick, Roger Federer was handed the Centre Court net as a memento by the All England Club (Rafael Nadal had asked for and been given the net after defeating Federer in the previous year's final). When questioned what he planned to do with it, Federer told journalists, 'Dunno. Probably one day in my chalet in Switzerland maybe I'll hang it against the wall or something.'

CHALLENGE CUP

The trophy presented to winners of the Wimbledon Men's Singles final is called the Challenge Cup. Standing 18 inches high and made of silver gilt, it carries the following inscription:

The All England
Lawn Tennis Club
Single Handed
Championship
of the World

The Challenge Cup has been handed to winners of the Men's final since 1887, the All England Club splashing out 100 guineas for it from the profits of the previous year's tournament. The trophy replaced another Challenge Cup which was purchased in 1883 but given permanently to William Renshaw after he won the competition three times in a row (1884–6). Prior to that there was another trophy, the Field Cup, which did the honours from 1877 to 1883. This also ended up in William Renshaw's hands after he became Men's Singles Champion in 1881, 1882 and 1883, so you can kind of understand why the All England Club now keeps the present Challenge Cup no matter how many times a player is crowned Wimbledon Champion.

ROSEWATER DISH

The trophy presented to winners of the Women's Singles final at Wimbledon is officially called the Ladies' Singles Plate, although it's more commonly known as the 'Rosewater Dish' or 'Venus Rosewater Dish'. The trophy carries no inscription other than the names of all previous champions although the artwork on this silver salver would give the ceiling of the Sistine Chapel a run for its money, with numerous mythical gods and goddesses depicted. That old chestnut about the trophy being named after Venus Williams because she kept winning the thing is, of course, nothing but an urban myth.

HERO TO ZERO

Suzanne Lenglen had all the attributes a tennis player could ever wish for – pace, perfect racquet control, excellent mobility and a ruthless streak a mile long. She won Wimbledon in 1919, 1920, 1921, 1922, 1923 and 1925, changing the public's perception of women's tennis in the process. And she did it with style, dressing in the shortest of skirts (at least by 1920s standards) while leaping around the court like a ballerina. Men flocked to see the French girl in action. She wasn't what you might call a beauty yet her tennis skills and electric personality meant Lenglen was the undisputed star of the Wimbledon show. All of which made what happened during the 1926 Championships even harder to bear. A scheduling mix-up meant Lenglen failed to show for a Centre Court match attended by Queen Mary. The crowd regarded this as an almighty slight to royalty and turned on her. With accusations of French arrogance flying around and tournament referee Frank Burrow insisting she knew perfectly well what time the match was supposed to start, Lenglen stormed out of Wimbledon in a huff and never returned. She died of anaemia in July 1938 at the age of just 39, two days after Helen Wills Moody, Lenglen's successor to the Women's throne, had won her eighth Wimbledon Singles title.

KING FOR A DAY

In terms of titles won at Wimbledon the Californian Elizabeth 'Bunny' Ryan is still right up there with the very best. Ryan carried off 19 titles between the years 1914 and 1934, all of them in Doubles competitions, a record that stood until Billie Jean King arrived on the scene. King equalled Ryan's feat in 1975 and, come the 1979 Championships, was closing in on a record twentieth title by making good progress with Martina Navratilova in the Women's Doubles event. 'I hope I never live to see my record broken,' Ryan had said earlier in the year when asked about her place in the Wimbledon history books. Her wish would be granted but under the most unfortunate of circumstances. On the second Friday of the Championships, Ryan collapsed while visiting the changing rooms at the All England Club and was pronounced dead on arrival at hospital. Twenty-four hours later King broke Ryan's long-standing record, partnering Navratilova to victory over Betty Stöve and Wendy Turnbull in the Women's Doubles final.

SEX CHANGE

Ever since anyone can remember women have always been referred to as Miss or Mrs on Wimbledon's scoreboards. That is until the 2009 Championships when the All England Club, to the horror of tennis traditionalists, decided to drop the prefixes in the name of political correctness. This led to widespread confusion with some spectators unsure whether they were about to watch a match involving men or women, while umpires stuck to their guns by continuing to refer to ladies as Mrs or Miss when announcing the scores. Even the players seemed unimpressed by the change. 'It's a shame,' said Laura Robson, defending Champion in the Girls' Singles event. 'I rather liked seeing "Miss" next to my name.'

KIDS' STUFF

The origins of Junior Wimbledon date back to 1947 when the All England Club invited some of the world's most gifted young players to attend the second week of the Championships, playing matches during the mornings before watching the grown-ups do their stuff in the afternoons. Today Junior Wimbledon operates pretty much along the same lines as the adult version of the tournament. Matches take place on the grass courts with players (aged 18 and under) competing over the best of three sets in Singles and Doubles events. Unfortunately, surprisingly few of them go on to make an impact as established professionals. There are exceptions – Pat Cash, Stefan Edberg and Martina Hingis among them – yet most fall by the wayside and are never heard of again. Scroll down the lists of previous Junior Wimbledon competitors and the vast majority of names will mean nothing to 99 per cent of sports writers, let along the average armchair tennis fan.

PRINCE OF WALES

For years people often confused Junior Wimbledon with the Junior Championships of Great Britain, a completely separate event that used to take place at the All England Club outside the Championship fortnight. In 1966 this tournament was famously won by J.P.R. Williams, later to become a key member of the all-conquering Welsh rugby union side of the 1970s, who beat David Lloyd in the final. 'There was quite a big crowd there, around 1,000 people,' Williams told yours truly in 2005. 'I wasn't really given a chance but I won 6–4, 6–4. It was very unreal. I remember my main worry was whether I'd be able to climb over the net at the end. Afterwards I went out with some mates and we drove around London. It didn't sink in until the following day what had happened.'

WELSH RAREBIT

Although tennis is one of the few sports than can be considered truly global, some countries undoubtedly have better track records at it than others. Despite the best efforts of the young J.P.R. Williams, Wales has never exactly set the tennis world on fire. In fact only one player from the Principality has to date ever appeared in a Wimbledon final – and he lost. That was Mike Davies from Swansea (later to become General Manager of the International Tennis Federation) who collected a runners-up medal from the 1960 Men's Doubles final.

DON'T CRY FOR ME

Despite producing a surprisingly high number of world class players from a relatively limited playing base, only one Argentinian has ever won a title at Wimbledon. That was Gabriela Sabatini who partnered Steffi Graf to victory in the 1988 Women's Doubles competition. Sabatini also finished runner-up in the Singles to Graf in 1990, a feat equalled in the men's game by her compatriot David Nalbandian who lost the 2002 final to Lleyton Hewitt.

DEVON KNOWS

The first overseas player to win a title at Wimbledon was May Sutton of the USA who defeated Dorothea Douglass 6–3, 6–4 in the 1905 Women's Singles final. Ah ha, but wait! Sutton's father was actually a captain in the Royal Navy and she herself was born in Plymouth, so you can't blame the good people of Devon for claiming her as their own.

FOREIGN LEGION

The first overseas players ever to compete at Wimbledon were James Dwight, Arthur Rives and Richard Sears, all from the USA, who took part in the 1884 Championships at Worple Road.

ALL THE SEVENS

Today Boris Becker is perhaps best known to anyone under the age of 35 as the man who fathered a child inside a broom cupboard at a Japanese restaurant in London. And yet back in 1985 the man was a tennis revelation, winning Wimbledon on the seventh day of the seventh month at the age of 17 years and 7 months to become by some distance the youngest Men's Champion ever. To be fair, Becker had given us fair warning of what lay in store. The previous year at Wimbledon he had been forced to retire from a fourth-round tie against Bill Scanlon after falling awkwardly (one journalist who visited Becker at his hotel that evening found him sat in a chair working out what his world ranking would have been had he won). In June 1985 he won the Stella Artois tournament at Queen's Club, the traditional men's precursor to Wimbledon, an indication if ever there was one that he would be a threat at the All England Club despite being unseeded. Over the course of two weeks and seven matches that summer Becker became a household name, winning Wimbledon thanks in part to his phenomenal serve and all-action style of play that had him diving full length around the court. But it was a close run thing. In the third round Joakim

Nystrom of Sweden twice served for the match against the German boy-wonder, while Tim Mayotte was two points from victory in their fourth-round tie. Becker's remarkable resilience saw him through on both occasions and he went on to defeat Kevin Curren in the final, becoming the first unseeded player – and the first German – ever to win Wimbledon. As if to prove it hadn't all been a fluke Becker returned the following year and won it again, disposing of Ivan Lendl in straight sets in the final.

UPSETS

Every year the Championships produce a number of surprise results, some more eye-catching than others. Here are 10 of Wimbledon's biggest post-war upsets:

Peter Doohan defeats Boris Becker, 1987

Becker had won Wimbledon in 1985 and 1986, Doohan was unheard of outside his native Australia. Surely there was only going to be one outcome, right? Wrong.

Ivo Karlovic defeats Lleyton Hewitt, 2003

Hewitt was the reigning Wimbledon Champion and number one seed while Karlovic, ranked 203 in the world, had to go through qualifying to earn a place in the main draw. Never before had a defending Men's Champion lost in the first round.

Lori McNeil defeats Steffi Graf, 1994

The first time a defending Women's Champion had ever lost in the first round.

Roger Taylor defeats Rod Laver, 1970

Laver was unbeaten at Wimbledon since July 1960 and had won all four Grand Slam events during 1969. This fourth-round defeat (to a Brit!) proved to be the beginning of the end for the legendary 'Rocket'.

Jelena Dokic defeats Martina Hingis, 1999

Hingis was the world number one and 1997 Wimbledon Champion, and yet she lost to a 16-year-old qualifier in the first round.

Richard Krajicek defeats Pete Sampras, 1996

Krajicek was a decent player but no one seriously expected him to defeat the all-conquering Sampras, Wimbledon winner in each of the previous three years. Sampras lost this quarter-final in straight sets, his only defeat at SW19 between July 1992 and June 2001. Krajicek went on to win the title.

Kevin Curren defeats John McEnroe, 1985

Like Krajicek, Curren was a more than useful player. McEnroe, however, was McEnroe. And yet Curren absolutely destroyed the three times Wimbledon Champion at the quarter-final stage, going on to make the final where he lost to Boris Becker.

Kathy Jordan defeats Chris Evert, 1983

Evert made it through to the last four at Wimbledon in all bar one of her 19 Championships spanning 1972 to 1989, losing to Jordan in the third round.

Charlie Fancutt defeats Ivan Lendl, 1981
Fancutt's 15 minutes of fame as the unknown Australian beat the number four seed before returning to obscurity.

Vitas Gerulaitis defeats Arthur Ashe, 1976
Gerulaitis, who had never progressed beyond the second round at any Grand Slam event, put himself on the tennis map by fighting back from two sets down to beat the defending Wimbledon Champion.

CASTLE RUINS

It may have escaped your attention but Andrew Castle – you know, the TV presenter, nice manner on the sofa in the mornings – was once a handy tennis player who in 1986 came close to springing a major surprise at Wimbledon against Mats Wilander. Castle led 2–1 in sets in front of a patriotic crowd on Court 1 before eventually succumbing 6–4, 6–7, 7–6, 4–6, 0–6 to the number two seed. His television commitments now include two weeks each year working at Wimbledon for the BBC where he is regarded as one of their better tennis summarisers.

THE GRAVEYARD

Okay, pay attention, this is going to get slightly confusing. For decades Court 2 at Wimbledon was known as 'The Graveyard', not because there were bodies buried beneath the turf but due to the extraordinary number of upsets that used to occur there. It was the place all the top players hated playing, where the stands were so close they were virtually on top of the court. If a seed was allocated a match on Court 2 then there was a fair chance they were going out of the tournament, which is why so many of them used to moan about the 'indignity' of being made to play there. Then, in 2009, the All England Club unveiled a brand new Court 2, far less of a bear pit than its predecessor. In the process the old Court 2 became the new Court 3 meaning the death rate is bound to fall as fewer seeds will have to play there. Which is a shame, as there's nothing more satisfying at Wimbledon than watching a multi-millionaire being mauled by a cash-strapped underdog.

COUNTING COURTS

The number of courts at Wimbledon has increased gradually over the years. In 2010 there were 19 varying in size from the Centre Court (capacity 15,000 people) to, say, Courts 5 and 6 which have seating for only 120 but tend to attract battalions of passers-by who stand and watch the action. As a result you often get a far better view of play on the main show courts than you do on the outside courts unless, that is, you are tall, in which case happy days!

BIRD'S EYE VIEW

For as long as it is there many will regard the best spectator vantage point at the All England Club to be the ridge adjoining the back row of seats on Courts 3 and

4. From here you can watch the action on both courts while also taking in matches on the surrounding Courts 5, 9 and 10. But beware – seating is only available on a first come, first served basis so be prepared to run for it once Wimbledon's entrance gates have opened, otherwise you're likely to be disappointed.

CENTRE STAGE

More people can fit inside the average lower league football ground than Wimbledon's Centre Court. And yet the All England Club's premier stage is still regarded as one of the finest sporting arenas in the world. The place is steeped in history, a legacy of the thousands of showpiece matches that have been played there since construction work was completed in 1922. Part of its aura is down to the almost regimental etiquette that surrounds the court, from the formality of the Royal Box to the strict code of silence that exists while rallies are in progress (something that contrasts wildly with, say, the pop concert atmosphere of the Arthur Ashe Stadium at the US Open). Things used to get slightly more rowdy when there were standing areas on the Centre Court. Despite being a lot of fun these were in hindsight an accident waiting to happen. On especially hot days spectators would frequently pass out yet remain upright, their lifeless bodies supported by the sheer volume of people pressed in around them. Only once the crowds began to thin would they fall to the floor before being carted off to the nearest first aid room. In 1990, following the tragic football disasters at Bradford and Hillsborough, these standing areas were ripped out in accordance with new safety legislation governing sports venues and replaced with extra seating. All Wimbledon finals are scheduled to be played on the Centre Court although a backlog in matches created by wet weather can occasionally result in some being switched elsewhere. Every player who comes to Wimbledon wants to appear on the Centre Court. The same applies to all the umpires, line judges, ball boys, ball girls and streakers. Yes, streakers.

THE NAKED TRUTH

The first streaker to 'grace' the Centre Court turf was Melissa Johnson, then 23, a Manchester University graduate who revealed all just as Richard Krajicek and MaliVai Washington prepared to face-off in the 1996 Men's final. Krajicek later admitted that Johnson's graceful dash had helped him relax (who needs tennis coaches or sports psychologists when the sight of bare flesh can cure any big match nerves?). Lleyton Hewitt and David Nalbandian had to put up with a naked man during their 2002 final while another male, a Dutch disc jockey by the name of Sander Lantinga, went starkers on Centre Court during the second set of Maria Sharapova's 2006 quarter-final win over Elena Dementieva. Other non-naked Centre Court intruders down the years have included:

The mouse which interrupted play between Yevgeny Kafelnikov and Mark Philippoussis in 1998.

Two racquet-carrying members of the Real Fathers For Justice pressure group who managed to hit a ball over the net a couple of times during Roger Federer's 2006 win over Mario Ancic before being escorted away.

The girl who ran on court during Ilie Nastase's 1974 clash with Jiri Hrebec, Nastase signing an autograph for the invader before she was led away by a member of London's law enforcement community.

The bird, believed to be a pied wagtail, which repeatedly interrupted matches during the second week of the 1990 Championships.

The swarm of bees which dive-bombed poor Kathy Rinaldi and Pam Shriver in 1982, the unfortunate Rinaldi being stung in the process.

Helen Jarvis from Surrey who staged a demonstration in favour of a new world banking system during the 1957 Men's Doubles final – as you do.

The pigeon which added to Tim Henman's woes during his 1999 semi-final against Pete Sampras, ruining the British number one's concentration during a vital service game by ambling around the court and stubbornly refusing to bugger off.

WHITE RIOT

The Centre Court. A place of decorum, respectability and best behaviour. Unless that is you happened to be there on Tuesday 30 June 1981, watching Sue Barker and Ann Kiyomura take on Jo Anne Russell and Virginia Ruzici in the third round of the Women's Doubles. Although the match had started a little after 7 p.m. the clear blue summer skies gave every indication that it would be completed before darkness fell, especially when Barker and Kiyomura went 5–3 down in the second set having already lost the opener 6–4. Then the fightback began. Barker and her American partner ended up taking the second on a tie-break by which time the stands were rapidly filling with punters keen to see more tennis and throw their weight behind the popular Brit. By the time it got to 5–5 in the third the light was fading slightly. With no tie-break to come in what was the deciding set, tournament referee Fred Hoyles appeared on court and called play off at 9.35 p.m. At which point all hell broke loose. First boos and jeers rang out. Then paper cups and programmes began raining down on the turf followed by a barrage of leather seat covers, the kind spectators can hire on arrival at Wimbledon to fight off 'numb bum' syndrome. When it became clear the players weren't going to return the stands gradually began to empty leaving behind a court covered in debris, bringing to an end the nearest thing Wimbledon has ever had to a riot. Play resumed again the following day and went on for another six fairly lengthy games, proof if it were needed that Hoyles had been right to pull the plug. The eventual winners? Barker and Kiyomura.

IF

'If you can meet with triumph and disaster
And treat those two imposters just the same'

Those 16 words, taken from the Rudyard Kipling poem 'If', are inscribed over the players' entrance to the Centre Court. They have been there since 1923, albeit on different boards (the original was replaced in 1995, a third making an appearance in 2002). They are the last words a player sees before entering the arena. Or, in Ilie Nastase's case, the first words he saw after beating Raul Ramirez in the pair's 1976 Men's semi-final. Irritated throughout the match by the whirring sound of cameras belonging to press photographers, Nastase decided to walk backwards off court so that his tormentors would be unable to take pictures of his face. Of course it had the exact reverse effect, Nastase's alternative exit becoming *the* story. Years later he confessed to taking a thermos flask of tea on court with him that day to help his body temperature match that of the sweltering conditions. How very British, especially for a Romanian.

FIRST SERVE

The first match ever to be played on Wimbledon's Centre Court took place on 26 June 1922 after King George V had declared the new Church Road grounds open by striking a gong three times. Needless to say the start was delayed by rain, Leslie Godfree and Algernon Kingscote finally getting proceedings underway at 3.30 p.m.

instead of 2.45 p.m. Godfree served the first point which Kingscote netted, prompting Godfree to run forward and pocket the ball as a souvenir.

ROYAL BOX

In 2005 a London University study revealed that it was easier to gain entry to any casino bank vault in Las Vegas than Wimbledon's Royal Box. Alright, that's a lie, but you get my drift. Unless you are royalty, an All England Club committee member (and that includes Cliff Richard), Terry Wogan, Michael Parkinson, Bruce Forsyth or a gold medal-winning British Olympian then you're not going to get in. For the record, Wimbledon's 75-seat Royal Box has overlooked the Centre Court since the grounds were opened in 1922. Dress is 'smart' which means no jeans, cowboy boots, Aston Villa replica football shirts or 'hoodie' attire. Hats are also out, even tasteful ones of the Ascot variety, to prevent obscuring the view of other people in the Royal Box. Invitations, not that the likes of you or me will ever receive one, come from the Chairman of the All England Club who considers suggestions from other committee members. Still, I'm not bitter. I'd rather be wedged between two boisterous, tipsy Australian lasses than Wogan and 'Parky' any day.

GETTING THERE – THE PUBLIC

Transport won't be a problem if you're a member of the Royal Box brigade – how painful can travelling in a chauffeur-driven Bentley possibly be? However, for us mere mortals getting to and coming from Wimbledon can be a bit more problematic. Driving is an option but then you're faced with M25-style traffic jams and parking charges that make sending your offspring to Eton seem extremely affordable. For thousands of punters the sensible option is the train. Here you've got two options – travel by the District Line tube route and alight at either Southfields or Wimbledon Park, or catch a train to Wimbledon main line station and take a bus or taxi the last couple of miles from there. This makes perfect sense until, say, 7.30 p.m. when in the middle of some titanic match on Court 1 you realise that the last train to Weymouth via Basingstoke leaves in 20 minutes time. What do you do? Get up and go or stay and miss your train? Every year during Wimbledon fortnight countless TV and radio commentators lay into the public for leaving matches early, carping on about the number of empty seats and players slogging their guts out for fans who don't care. The only reason these poor souls quit is because they don't want to spend the night on Wimbledon station waiting for the first train to Yeovil Junction the next morning. John McEnroe please take note – unlike New York City, Britain doesn't have a 24/7 public transport system.

GETTING THERE – THE PLAYERS

Most of the players competing at Wimbledon each year take advantage of a fleet of chauffeur-driven courtesy cars that collect and return them to wherever they happen to be staying during the Championships. Some, however, choose alternative means of getting to and from the All England Club. For those rich enough to afford to rent lush properties nearby, walking is an option (albeit nearly always escorted by burly security guards). Then there was Martina Navratilova who sometimes cycled to work, using the journey as part of her warm up/warm down routine. Before relocating to Church Road many tennis players also took advantage of the railway halt next to the grounds at Worple Road, travelling on trains surrounded by the same people who watched them compete.

MOVING PICTURES

Thanks to television the vast majority of people who follow Wimbledon do so from the comfort of their own living room, thereby avoiding any headaches over the cost of parking, last trains, etc. The first ever televised play happened in 1937 when the BBC, using two cameras at opposite ends of the Centre Court, broadcast 25 minutes of the match between Henry 'Bunny' Austin and George Lyttleton Rogers (the only problem being that hardly anyone had a TV to watch it on). It wasn't until 1967 that the first colour transmission took place, BBC2 showing Roger Taylor's clash against Cliff Drysdale in its entirety. For 12 years (1956–68) independent television also covered Wimbledon, only to realise that it made no commercial sense whatsoever screening exactly the same pictures as the BBC. Now there are cameras all over the All England Club. In fact the advent of interactive TV means you get to see far more action at home than you would if you were actually there. No wonder the Broadcast Centre at Wimbledon is officially recognised as the largest outside broadcast facility in the world. As a result more people watch Wimbledon on TV than any other tennis tournament.

'THAT' PIECE OF MUSIC

'Da da, da da da da dada, da da da da DAA'

Oh come on, you must recognise it! The piece of music that the BBC has used to introduce Wimbledon TV programmes since way back in the 1970s. It is actually called 'Light And Tuneful' and was written specifically to accompany the BBC's Wimbledon coverage by Keith Mansfield, the man who also composed the theme tune to the long running Saturday afternoon sports show *Grandstand*. As for the military sounding music which traditionally ends each BBC TV transmission from Wimbledon, well that's called 'Sporting Occasion'. It was written by the late Major Leslie Statham, Director of Music of the Band of the Welsh Guards, who traded under the name Arnold Steck.

TANNER'S FIVE MINUTES

The All England Club is famous for running the Wimbledon Championships with almost military precision. It also respects tradition. When the American NBC television network asked in 1979 if the start of the Men's final between Björn Borg and Tennessee's Roscoe Tanner could be put back from 2 p.m. to 2.05 p.m. in order to accommodate adverts and introductory titles, there was only ever going to be one answer – forget it. Not to be dissuaded, NBC went away and had a quiet word with Tanner. Sure enough as the Centre Court clock ticked round to 2 p.m. on 7 July, Tanner asked for and was granted permission to take a toilet break during the closing stages of his on-court warm up with Borg. Four minutes later he returned and at 2.05 p.m. precisely the Men's final got underway, millions stateside managing to catch every ball of all five sets. Not that it did the scheming Americans any good though, Borg triumphing 6–7, 6–1, 3–6, 6–3, 6–4 to claim his fourth consecutive Wimbledon Singles title.

TIE-BREAK OF TIE-BREAKS

Björn Borg returned to the All England Club in 1980 to win his fifth consecutive Singles title, beating John McEnroe in the final. It was this match that contained the most memorable tie-break in Wimbledon history. Tie-breaks had been introduced at major tennis tournaments during the early 1970s (1971 in the All England Club's case) as a way of stopping sets going on forever. The 1980 final saw McEnroe comfortably take the opening set 6–1 only for Borg to fight back and win the next two. Come the end of the fourth set with the scores level at 6–6 the tie-break came into operation. Today surprisingly few people actually remember who won the tie-break. They just recall that it went on and on with both men playing the tennis of their lives. For the record it finished 18–16 in McEnroe's favour after Borg had wasted five match points, the Swede eventually triumphing 8–6 in the fifth and final set to win the penultimate Grand Slam title of his career.

DO THE STRAND

On the final evening of the tournament after the last matches have been played, everyone retires to the Champions' Dinner in central London to toast the winners, console the losers and generally let their hair down. This event always used to take place at the Savoy Hotel on The Strand though the venue has recently switched to the Intercontinental on Park Lane. In reality few of the players who have just competed at Wimbledon attend as most leave London the moment they are knocked out of the competition. That means that the dinner tends to be rammed with tennis officials and Wimbledon committee members interspersed with the odd finalist. Until recently the respective Singles Champions were always expected to dance together. Sadly this long-held tradition has been given the heave-ho, although no one seems to know why. Maybe it's because the players kept turning up late. In 2008 most of the food and drink had disappeared well before Rafael Nadal made it through the door at 1 a.m. such was the length of his match against Roger Federer. It was much the same story the following year, Federer showing up around midnight after his marathon final with Andy Roddick.

SUPERBRAT

In 1981 John McEnroe ducked out of the Champions' Dinner having won the Men's final earlier that day, ending Björn Borg's run of five consecutive Wimbledon titles. McEnroe's notoriously fiery temper had hit new heights (or lows, depending on your point of view) during the tournament, the absolute nadir being his infamous 'You cannot be serious'/'You guys are the absolute pits of the world' rant at umpire Edward James during a torrid first-round match against Tom Gullikson. It was this meltdown which spawned a hit single ('Chalk Dust – The Umpire Strikes Back' by Brat which reached number 19 in the British charts) and gave McEnroe the title for his 2002 autobiography (*You Cannot Be Serious*, shortened to *Serious* for its European release). Superbrat's non-attendance at the Champions' Dinner proved to be the last straw and for the first time the All England Club chose not to make their new Champion an honorary member. Twelve months later McEnroe was finally offered membership even though he lost the 1982 Men's final to Jimmy Connors.

FINAL DAYS

If you're reading this thinking, 'I swear the Men's final always used to be on a Saturday,' then congratulations, because it did. Between 1969 and 1981 the Men's final took place on the second Saturday of the tournament with the Women's Champion having being crowned the day before (between 1933 and 1969 it was the other way round, the men playing on the Friday while the women entertained on Saturday). Ever since 1982 the Women's final has been scheduled for the Saturday, the Men's 24 hours later. That means the Championships, weather of course depending, now spans 13 playing days as opposed to 12 allowing more time for the vast number of matches to be completed.

PEOPLE'S SUNDAY

It has always been the case that the middle Sunday of the Championships is set aside for rest, with no competitive matches taking place. However, the British weather being what it is, occasionally tradition has to be thrown out of the window. The first time play took place on a middle Sunday was in 1991 when one of the wettest first weeks ever left the All England Club with no option but to open its doors on the Sabbath. What came to be dubbed 'People's Sunday' proved to be a huge success as people queued for tickets on a first come, first served basis, creating a carnival atmosphere once inside with their 'Mexican waves' and football-style chanting. Even Jimmy Connors said he'd never known an atmosphere like it, his every strike of the ball in the warm-up with third-round opponent Derrick Rostagno being cheered to the Centre Court rafters. More first week wash-outs led to repeats of 'People's Sunday' in 1997 and 2004.

SONGS OF PRAISE

One of the more bizarre Sundays in Wimbledon history occurred on 1 June 1997. To celebrate the completion of the new Court 1 – and as a way of giving it a test run – the All England Club allowed the BBC to record an episode of the religious show *Songs Of Praise* inside the arena. Around 9,000 people attended, the vast majority belonging to churches in the south London/north Surrey areas. The show was screened four weeks later on the middle Sunday of the 1997 Championships.

DOUBLE TROUBLE

There's a fair chance that Maria de Amorin of Brazil prayed for some kind of divine intervention during her second-round Singles tie against Berna Thung at Wimbledon in 1957. Having been given a bye in the opening round, de Amorin started appallingly by serving four consecutive double faults, Thung winning the game without even striking a ball. And so it went on. All told, the Brazilian hit 17 consecutive double faults – that's 34 serves missing the target – before finally landing one in. Painful isn't the word. Incredibly, de Amorin was doing okay on her return of serve and managed to break three times during the first set before finally succumbing 6–3. After that she recovered her composure to take the second set 6–4 before falling apart once again in the deciding third, losing 6–1. 'I was very nervous,' de Amorin admitted during the post-match press conference, the only saving grace being that no TV cameras were on Court 6 to record her nightmare.

FLIPPING HECK!

There was little to separate Frank Riseley and Sydney Smith as the two men went head to head in the fifth round at Wimbledon in 1904. With the score delicately poised at two sets all the pair decided on a novel way of determining their fate – they would flip a coin. Riseley won and ended up progressing to the final where he lost in straight sets to Hugh Doherty. This remains the only known occasion where a match at Wimbledon has been decided on the toss of a coin. Why did they do it? Because Riseley and Smith were also a pair in the Men's Doubles and wanted to preserve some energy for that competition.

RAIN MAN

Take a sport that requires anything between 45 minutes and 5 hours to complete a match. Then try and play it in a country where rain falls incessantly, even during the summer time. Is it any surprise that so many matches at Wimbledon get suspended due to the wet stuff? The arrival of rain during a match can be a blessing or a curse for a tennis player. If you're performing badly and in danger of being soundly beaten, it can buy you time to get your act together. And vice versa. In 2001 Tim Henman was leading Goran Ivanisevic by two sets to one and two games to one in the pair's semi-final clash when rain forced the players off court. The following day Ivanisevic recovered to take the fourth set, establishing a 3–2 lead in the decider before rain again intervened. On day three the Croatian required just 18 minutes to finish off Britain's number one. Had the rain not arrived midway through that fourth set then Henman would probably have reached the final and Ivanisevic's name wouldn't now be on the roll call of Men's Singles Champions. What everyone forgets is that Tim had himself been rescued in the fourth round that year by Wimbledon's wonky climate. Two sets to one down against the American Todd Martin and struggling with a back spasm, Henman was on his way out of the tournament when a spot of drizzle allied with fading light saw the game halted until the following day. Twenty-four hours later Henman returned having received treatment for his ailing back and, hey presto, reeled off the next two sets to book a place in the quarter-finals. Had there been a roof on the Centre Court back in 2001, then Martin would almost certainly have won.

HENMAN HILL

Tim Henman's 2001 showdown with Goran Ivanisevic was just one of four Wimbledon semi-finals for the popular Brit. He lost each time (1998, 1999, 2001, 2002) but the interest stirred by his exploits was considerable with huge crowds converging on SW19 to watch him play. Those without tickets for the matches but desperate to be close(ish) to the action congregated around a giant TV screen situated opposite a large grass bank officially known as the Aorangi Terrace. During the 2001 Championships BBC sports presenter Sue Barker referred to it as 'Henman Hill', the frantic atmosphere there frequently surpassing that around whatever court he happened to be playing on (usually the Centre Court). Since Henman's retirement attempts have been made by the media to rename the bank in honour of Andy Murray (Murray Mound, Murray Mountain, Mount Murray) and Laura Robson (Robson Green). However, in most people's eyes – including those of Murray – it will always be 'Henman Hill'. As Henman himself said during an appearance on the TV show *Friday Night With Jonathan Ross*, 'He (Murray) can have all those Grand Slams he's going to win but I'm keeping my hill.'

GENE GENIE

Tim Henman had it in his genes to be a tennis player. His great-grandmother, Ellen Stawell-Brown, was one of the first women to serve over-arm at Wimbledon while grandfather Henry Billington competed at the Championships after the Second World War. Henman's grandmother, Susan Billington, was also the last woman to regularly serve underarm at Wimbledon between 1946 and 1956.

DUMB WIMBLEDON

Tim Henman was usually one of the more co-operative players when it came to the media, politely handling multiple requests for interviews both in the run-up to Wimbledon and during the Championships. Others can be more reluctant when it comes to press, radio and TV demands, understandably so when you consider some of the bizarre questions and statements (often from the tabloid press) that come their way during the tournament, a list that includes:

'Can I ask you about your knickers?'

To Tatiana Golovin of France, 2007

'Apart from tennis, do you have any special abilities or party tricks you're able to pull out when you're not on court?'

To Justine Henin, 2007

'Serena, you don't look happy at all.'

To Serena Williams after she had lost the 2008 final

'Ivo, how come you are so tall?'
To 6ft 10in Ivo Karlovic, 2003

'Have you ever been to Devon?'
To Andy Murray, 2006

'What's your favourite drink?'
**To Janko Tipsarevic of Serbia after being asked if he knew
what 'Tipsy' means in English, which in turn followed him
talking eloquently about his country's war-torn past**

'What's your favourite Michael Jackson song?'
To various players, 2009, the day after Jackson's death

Ironically one of Wimbledon's most famous press conference 'strops' was thrown by a player facing legitimate (rather than stupid) questions posed by a television journalist. In 2002 Anna Kournikova, struggling to live up to her early career promise, was asked by the BBC's Garry Richardson if she had considered taking a step down to play in second tier 'Challenger' tournaments in order to get her game back on track, something Andre Agassi did with tremendous results during 1998. Kournikova took exception and tried to leave the TV studio before being persuaded to return and answer questions purely about the first-round match she had just lost rather than her stagnating career. To say the piece that aired across Britain that evening had a 'frosty' feel about it would be an understatement of colossal proportions. 'I've been conducting interviews at Wimbledon for 22 years and in that time have spoken to (Jimmy) Connors and (John) McEnroe, and no one has ever tried to walk out before,' said Richardson of the altercation.

MOTHER RUSSIA

Whereas the not entirely unattractive Anna Kournikova quit tennis prematurely without ever reaching a Grand Slam final, it wasn't long before another blonde bombshell of Russian descent arrived to take her place. This time the girl with the pin-up looks had substance as well as style. In 2004 Maria Sharapova, aged 17 years and 75 days, became the third youngest Wimbledon Women's Singles Champion ever, defeating Serena Williams in the final 6–1, 6–4. Before receiving the trophy from the Duke of Kent, Sharapova called her mother Yelena (who was on board a plane touching down in New York) to deliver the good news, the first time a player had ever used a mobile phone while on the Centre Court.

NUMBER CRUNCHING

Youngest Wimbledon Men's Singles Champion
Boris Becker (1985), 17 years and 227 days

Youngest Wimbledon Women's Singles Champion
Charlotte 'Lottie' Dod (1887), 15 years and 285 days

Oldest Wimbledon Men's Singles Champion
Arthur Gore (1909), 41 years and 182 days

Oldest Wimbledon Women's Singles Champion
Charlotte Sterry (1908), 37 years and 282 days

Youngest Male Competitor
Sidney Wood (1927), 15 years and 231 days

Youngest Female Competitor
Jennifer Capriati (1990), 14 years and 90 days

Tallest Male Competitor
Ivo Karlovic, 6ft 10in

Shortest Male Competitor
Felicisimo Ampon, 4ft 11in

Tallest Female Competitor
Lisa Davenport and Elena Bovina, both 6ft 2½in

Shortest Female Competitor
Gertrude Hoahing, 4ft 9½in

SIT DOWN

It used to be the case that players had to stand up during the change of end breaks at Wimbledon, loitering with intent around the umpire's chair waiting for the man (and it was always a man back then) to call time. In 1975 the All England Club provided chairs on all courts for competitors to use, something that has continued ever since. Amazingly one of the chief reservations within tennis governing circles about introducing chairs at tennis tournaments was that fatigued players might actually fall asleep on them while matches were still in progress.

OUT FOR LUNCH

You've got to feel sorry for poor Dorothy Cavis-Brown. Back in 1964 Roy Emerson won the Wimbledon Men's Singles title defeating Fred Stolle in the final, Maria Bueno of Brazil becoming Women's Champion for the third time. And yet all anyone seems to remember about the 1964 Championships is that line judge Mrs Cavis-Brown fell asleep when she should have been keeping an eye on the first-round match between South Africa's Abie Segal and Clark Graebner of the USA. Segal had won the first two sets on Court 3 and was serving at 5–2, match point in the third when an attempted pass by Graebner landed out. When the call of 'out' didn't come all eyes turned to Cavis-Brown who was sat fast asleep, arms folded with her head tilted sideways. 'The rules say that if nobody calls "out" the game isn't over,' Graebner told Segal as the pair stood at the net, bemused but at the same time amused by the situation. It was Segal who took decisive action, moving in on the sleeping figure to loudly ask, 'Hey madam, do you mind calling "out"!' At which point Cavis-Brown opened her eyes and said, 'out.' 'I always knew my game was boring but I didn't think it was that bad,' joked Segal afterwards. Cavis-Brown's take on her painfully public snooze? 'I think I became a little dizzy, a little drowsy. I have had a very exhausting time just lately,' she said, refusing to elaborate on rumours of a liquid lunch being responsible. Publicly the All England Club backed Cavis-Brown but she was never asked to call the lines at Wimbledon again.

'THE QUEUE'

Only in Britain would queueing up to see a sporting event become an integral part of the actual occasion itself. Being tennis, 'The Queue' – as the All England Club grandly refers to it – has a leisurely, warm feeling about it which is ridiculous really when you consider some people spend anything up to two days in the thing, camping out overnight in order to get the best tickets available. Its orderly nature borders on the sinister. Where else would thousands of people spend hour after hour waiting in line and yet not argue or bicker among themselves? In fact quite the opposite; lifelong friendships not to mention several weddings have resulted from complete strangers discovering each other in 'The Queue'. The lines of people are supposedly policed by officials who belong to the Association of Wimbledon Honorary Stewards. Most of these stewards are kind souls who will treat you like the honest, law-abiding human being that you are. Others, however, see 'The Queue' as their regimental sergeant major moment, barking out instructions like they're on a parade ground at Sandhurst. It is the behaviour of these aggressive stewards that bonds 'The Queue' together, fostering an 'us' versus 'them' atmosphere that verges on the politest form of mutiny known to mankind ('I most certainly will *not* move two feet to the left . . . oh alright then, seeing as though you said please').

CELEBRITY SPOTTING

Of course if you're a celebrity then you won't know about 'The Queue'. That's because managers and public relations people will secure tickets in advance so you don't have to spend 18 hours camped out in the rain next to the O'Grady family from Swindon. Not just any old tickets mind you, but good ones away from the riff raff – and the chances are someone else will pay or, even better, they'll be complimentary. Result! With every passing year more and more celebrities seem to drop in on Wimbledon. A glance around the Centre Court stands during the 2009 Men's Singles final revealed a right old assortment taking in the worlds of entertainment (Russell Crowe, Woody Allen), politics (Henry Kissinger) and sport (Sir Alex Ferguson, footballer Michael Ballack). The BBC even ran a lengthy interview with that well known authority on tennis Ben Stiller. In fact so many celebrities (plus partners) were present during the 2009 finals weekend that it's a wonder there was any room left for Mr and Mrs Normal. At least Mick Jones, formerly of The Clash, made no attempt to disguise the real reason behind his visit during the first week of that particular year's Championships. 'The tennis? Na. I'm here to party!' The party in question? A VIP star-studded event hosted by Evian, one of Wimbledon's sponsors. Honestly, it's alright for some.

'THE HOFF'

One of the more infamous celebrity visits to Wimbledon occurred in 2006 when David Hasselhoff of *Baywatch* fame dropped in on SW19. According to reports the actor was escorted from the grounds by security guards after behaving in a, how can I put it, 'tired and emotional' way. The All England Club did its best to play down the incident claiming 'The Hoff' had not been ejected after trying to enter a restricted area without the correct accreditation pass, but the press still had a field day. Whatever the truth, Hasselhoff has yet to return to Wimbledon.

THE CORPORATE GAME

Corporate hospitality. Two words that provoke wildly contrasting reactions in people. There are those who see it as an important way of maintaining and establishing work contacts outside the office over good food and fine wine. Others view the whole business as nothing more than an excuse for overpaid freeloaders to get drunk and devalue occasions with their arrogant, couldn't-care-less behaviour. Whatever your opinion, there's no escaping the fact that corporate hospitality figures prominently at major sporting events in Britain, Wimbledon included. Companies hand over vast sums of money to entertain clients and would-be clients in private marquees at the All England Club, those involved occasionally venturing out to watch a ball being hit. Some don't bother with the tennis at all. But then that's hardly unique to Wimbledon. How many times do you see expensive seats at major rugby and football matches go unoccupied after half-time because he/she has opted to prop up the free bar in a corporate box instead? Where do I stand on the subject? Whatever floats your boat is fine by me, unless of course you mention the Royal Bank of Scotland's decision to splash out £300,000 on corporate hospitality at Wimbledon in 2009 having just received £20 million in bail-outs from the taxpayer. That might just get me a bit hot under the collar.

DINING OUT

According to the All England Club, Wimbledon is 'the largest single annual sporting catering operation carried out in Europe.' How they know this is anyone's guess, but there's no denying that an awful lot of food and drink is consumed every year by those converging on the Championships. Over the course of the fortnight, the following quantities (approximately) are consumed:

32,000 portions of fish and chips
12,000 kilos of poached and smoked salmon
135,000 ice creams
190,000 sandwiches
150,000 bottles of water
22,000 slices of pizza
300,000 cups of tea and coffee
150,000 buns, scones, pastries and doughnuts
100,000 pints of lager and bitter
17,000 bottles of champagne
200,000 glasses of Pimms
30,000 litres of milk

STRAWBERRIES (AND CREAM)

Just as Morecambe went with Wise and Cagney goes with, er, Lacey, so the word Wimbledon fits hand-in-glove with strawberries and cream. Around 25,000 kilos of strawberries are consumed each year during the Championships, every one of them picked the previous day in Kent. The strawberries are then transported to Wimbledon and inspected for quality before going on sale. Around 7,000 litres of fresh cream is used to cover them. Why Kent? Because both the climate and the soil are perfect for growing strawberries – well, it's not known as the Garden of England for nothing. Almost as important is how much they cost. Over the years much has been made of the exorbitant prices charged at Wimbledon for strawberries and cream. In 2008 a punnet of 10 strawberries with cream cost £2.25. That compares with £2 in 2004, £1.80 in 2000 and £1.70 in 1993. Compared with the extortionate rise in the cost of living over the past couple of decades, that's not such a bad increase. Mind you, it could be argued they were way too expensive in the first place.

DISGUSTED

Discontent over the cost of food and drink on sale at Wimbledon is certainly nothing new. Back in 1914 the price of a cup of tea and a piece of cake at the All England Club's Worple Road grounds rose from five pence to six pence, prompting letters of complaint from disgusted of Tunbridge Wells types threatening never to set foot in the place again.

BALLS

Around 15,000 tennis balls are used on average each Wimbledon fortnight, another 6,000 being hit during the qualifying tournaments for the Championships. An additional 1,800 are used by players for practice purposes only. New balls are taken after the first seven games of a match, then after every subsequent nine. Many of these are later sold either to clubs affiliated to the Lawn Tennis Association or people attending the Championships. Yellow balls have been used at Wimbledon since 1986.

GAME, SET AND GRUNT

No one is sure exactly when it began, or even who started it. All we know is that it happens now all the time. What am I talking about? Grunting, that's what. If I were a betting man, I'd say the chief catalyst was probably Monica Seles who sounded as though she was giving birth rather than striking a tennis ball (Jennifer Capriati once went as far as telling her to 'Shut the * * * * up' during a match between the pair). Seles certainly opened the floodgates, making it 'acceptable' in the women's game. Since then countless females including the likes of Maria Sharapova and Serena Williams have done it. At times it seems as though they're trying to out-grunt rather than out-hit each other. So why do they do it? The guilty parties insist it is down to physical exertion. Their critics say it's an act of gamesmanship designed to put off opponents. In 2009 Michelle Larcher de Brito was handed a wildcard into Wimbledon a couple of weeks after making global headlines for her atomic grunting during a match at the French Open. With the sport's governing bodies threatening to get tough on excessive grunters, all eyes fell on the Portuguese girl amid talk that umpires at the Championships would dock points from the worst offenders. To nobody's great surprise Larcher de Brito managed to keep a lid on her vocals, though other more high profile players continued wailing as per usual throughout the tournament. The grunters might provide the tabloids with endless column inches every Wimbledon but as far as the majority of tennis followers are concerned grunting is, to quote Martina Navratilova, 'cheating, pure and simple.'

YOU WHAT?

'These ball boys are marvellous. You don't even notice them. There's a left-handed one over there. I noticed him earlier.'
Former BBC radio commentator Max Robertson

'Sure, I've been on the Tube. I caught one to Eastbourne once.'
Serena Williams on the ridiculously long new Northern Line extension

'Tim Henman's injured shoulder has raised its ugly head again.'
BBC Radio 5 Live commentator Jonathan Overend

'Here we see Andre Sa who, never having won a competitive match, has reached the Wimbledon quarter-final.'

John McEnroe

'I brought two hundred (headbands) with me and I've already given away about a hundred. I have no idea how many I have left.'

Pat Cash, Wimbledon, 1988

'Let's hope he can force him into those unforced errors.'

Tim Henman commentating at Wimbledon, 2008

'A lot of people think that everything revolves around Wimbledon but it is just one week of the year for us. If nothing happens at Wimbledon it's not the end of the world.'

Elena Baltacha shoots herself in the foot while attempting to defend Britain's poor record at Wimbledon, 2009

Andrew Castle: 'Where are all these Serbians from?'
Greg Rusedski: 'Serbia?'

BBC TV, Wimbledon, 2007

LUCKY LOSER

George Bastl was down and out. The American-born Swiss had just seen his dream of playing at the 2002 Wimbledon Championships go up in smoke, losing in the third round of the qualifying tournament at Roehampton to Alexander Waske of Germany. His bags were packed, the flight home booked. And then something strange happened. A gap appeared in the Men's Singles draw due to the late withdrawal of Spain's Felix Mantilla. Would, the All England Club wanted to know, George care to fill it as a lucky loser? Does the Pope have a balcony? So Bastl took his place in the first round and, playing with the carefree abandon of someone whose Christmas had come early, defeated Denis Golovanov in straight sets. Next up, Pete Sampras, the seven times Wimbledon Singles Champion. 'Pistol' Pete was supposedly past his prime but no one gave the man on the other side of the net a prayer, least of all Bastl himself. Well what do you know? To the amazement of the tennis world, Bastl triumphed 6–3, 6–2, 4–6, 3–6, 6–4, Pete's only consolation being that Andre Agassi also crashed out in the second round on a day of almighty shocks. Alas, round three proved to be a step too far as Bastl lost in straight sets to the competition's eventual runner-up, David Nalbandian. Still, a third-round loser's cheque for £21,260 helped soften the blow. As for Sampras? He never played at Wimbledon again.

SWISS HEIR

'The future has come today.' So said Boris Becker following Roger Federer's first Wimbledon Men's Singles title win in 2003. What hardly anyone remembers now is how close Federer came to defaulting from his fourth-round match that year, one of those classic 'What if?' scenarios which, had it come to pass, could have changed the passage of tennis history. While warming up on Court 2 with his opponent Feliciano Lopez of Spain,

Federer injured his back. 'At the time I just couldn't move, so I had to call the trainer I was in such a lot of pain,' he said afterwards. 'As the match went on it got a little better because your body gets warm. You try to forget that you are suffering as you get into the match.' His cause was helped by the Spaniard's curious failure to exploit Federer's lack of mobility, the Swiss legend-in-waiting somehow prevailing in straight sets. Had he been scheduled to play again the following day then there was every possibility Federer would have been forced to withdraw from the Championships. As it was he had 48 hours to recuperate before his quarter-final against Sjeng Schalken, time enough to receive treatment and recover adequately. And the rest, as they say, is . . .

JULIETTE BRAVO

On returning to Switzerland after his 2003 Wimbledon Men's Singles final victory over Mark Philippoussis, Roger Federer was presented with a cow by the organisers of a tournament in Gstaad, close to his home. Juliette was, so I've been told (and I'm no animal expert), a dairy cow belonging to the local Simmental breed. So whatever happened to her? Well it's not good news I'm afraid. According to the Australian tennis legend Roy Emerson, also a Gstaad resident, Juliette gave birth to a calf but subsequently stopped producing milk. And there's only one thing that tends to happen to cows that cease yielding milk – a one-way ticket to the abattoir. Emerson, it should be said, knows a thing or two about cows. He grew up on a dairy farm in Queensland.

STYLE COUNCIL

On the first day of the 1930 Championships a revolution took place at Wimbledon when the British player Brame Hillyard played his first-round Men's Singles match on Court 10 wearing . . . shorts! Cue multitudes of, 'Oh my word, you can see his legs!' -style comments. Would SW19 survive this daring break with tradition? Of course it would. Three years later Henry 'Bunny' Austin upped the stakes by donning shorts on the Centre Court that actually stopped above the knees. From that point on there was no going back. Change was in the air and the long trousers and ridiculous dresses that had been *de rigueur* on tennis courts the world over were consigned to the museum. The golden rule at Wimbledon tends to be that so long as a tennis player is dressed predominantly in white then it's acceptable. Even the risqué lace-edged panties exhibited in 1949 by 'Gorgeous' Gussie Moran passed the acid test. However, every once in a while someone will push the boat out too far. In 1985 Anne White of the USA famously played the opening instalment of her first-round match against Pam Shriver on Court 2 dressed in an all-white neck to ankle leotard. Rain meant the tie was completed the following day by which time tournament referee Alan Mills had advised White to wear something more appropriate ('I think I showed a lot of guts,' she later insisted). John McEnroe once tested the water by wearing black shorts onto the Centre Court only for Wimbledon's fashion police to nab him during the pre-match warm up while Rafael Nadal was warned in advance that his garish green vests would be a definite no-no (his 'pirate' trousers were however given the thumbs-up – providing they were white). A measure of how strict Wimbledon is on dress sense comes in the competition's official rules laid down by the All England Club – 'Any competitor who appears on court dressed in a manner deemed unsuitable by the Committee will be liable to be defaulted.' Budding stars of the future, you have been warned!

FLYING THE FLAG(S)

One of the more popular players to grace Wimbledon either side of the Second World War was Jaroslav Drobny, a talented left-hander born in Prague who became Men's Singles Champion in 1954. Bizarrely, Drobny competed at Wimbledon under four different nationalities during his long playing career. The war meant he became something of a wandering nomad, forsaking his Czech citizenship for that of Bohemia-Moravia (a German occupied rump of Czechoslovakia) before later accepting the offer of an Egyptian passport. It was as an Egyptian that he won Wimbledon though by that time his victory was greeted more like a British triumph, Drobny having married an English girl and settled in London. He later become a British citizen and competed as such in Veterans' Doubles competitions at the All England Club. Drobny died in Tooting, aged 79, in 2001 having remained a London resident for the rest of his life.

IVAN'S AGONY

Like Jaroslav Drobny, Ivan Lendl would forsake his Czechoslovakian nationality in favour of another country (in his case the USA). Lendl was desperate to win Wimbledon and everyone expected him one day to be crowned king of the Centre Court, hence his top seed status in 1986, 1988, 1989 and 1990. And yet Lendl would become one of those great players destined always to miss out on the ultimate prize. Fourteen times he came to Wimbledon, reaching the final in 1986 and 1987 when he lost to Boris Becker and Pat Cash respectively (there was also the heartbreak of five semi-final defeats along the way). Still, don't feel too sorry for Ivan as he managed to net over $21 million during a playing career that took in eight Grand Slam title wins (two at the Australian Open, three at the French Open, three at the US Open). The list of other Grand Slam Champions never to win Wimbledon includes such celebrated names as Ilie Nastase, Monica Seles, Ken Rosewall, Jennifer Capriati, Fred Stolle, Hana Mandlikova, Mats Wilander, Arantxa Sanchez-Vicario, Pat Rafter, Yevgeny Kafelnikov and Jim Courier.

NO SHOW GUSTAVO

If there is one thing Wimbledon buffs (and All England Club members) really hate it's when an extremely talented tennis player decides for no apparent reason that they can't be bothered turning up in SW19. Ninety-five per cent of those on the tennis tour would give their non-serving arm to play at Wimbledon, yet there are others for whom the Championship is far from the be all and end all. Take Gustavo Kuerten for instance. In June 2001 the Brazilian won the French Open to become the number one ranked player in the world. But instead of then heading to Wimbledon to consolidate his place at the top of the pile he opted out, much to the chagrin of seemingly everyone except the player himself. Okay, so Kuerten was a clay court specialist and not particularly fond of grass, but he'd still reached the third round the previous year. Surely the mark of any great champion is to try and be the best on all surfaces? Arguably the one beneficiary of Kuerten's no-show was Goran Ivanisevic, the eventual Men's Singles Champion that year. Had Kuerten taken his place in the draw then Ivanisevic might not have been granted his wildcard into the tournament, denying us one of the great sporting stories of modern times.

PUSHY PARENTS

If there has been a downside to the wonderful world of tennis over recent decades then the role of the overbearing pushy parent takes the biscuit. This has always tended to be more prevalent in the women's game with no end of players suffering mental as well as physical abuse at the hands of a dominant parent. Perhaps the worst of these offenders was Damir Dokic, father of Jelena Dokic. The outrageous public behaviour of this burly, bearded figure at tennis events frequently reduced his daughter to tears, Jelena severing all ties with her dad in 2002 because of what she later referred to as 'the situation'. During the

2000 Wimbledon Championships Damir Dokic had been escorted by police from the All England Club following a bout of disorderly (and allegedly drunk) behaviour, the sight of him being led away draped in the flag of St George sending shivers down the spines of all right-minded people present. Jelena probably wouldn't have made it to Wimbledon in the first place had it not been for Damir. And yet if it wasn't for Damir's behaviour then Jelena could well have achieved so much more in her career than one Grand Slam semi-final, that ironically coming just days after her father's ejection from Wimbledon.

WILD THINGS

While there is no shortage of pushy parents to be found at Wimbledon one thing you'll rarely see around the All England Club are pigeons. That's because every morning during the Championships birds of prey are flown in the grounds to scare them off. Recent Wimbledons have seen Rufus the Harris Hawk and Callisto the Peregrine Falcon on anti-pigeon duties, both owned and trained by Wayne Davis. For the record, Rufus tops the pecking order by keeping an eye on the Centre Court while Callisto patrols the wider skies above the club.

HARD GRAFT

If there's one thing Wimbledon would struggle to survive without, it's ball boys. Or rather ball boys and ball girls. Just imagine the likes of Ilie Nastase, John

McEnroe or Maria Sharapova scrambling around on their hands and knees before serving or, heaven forbid, having to fetch their own towels. Ball boys first appeared at the Championships during the 1920s when they were provided by the Shaftesbury children's homes. After the Second World War boys from Dr Barnardo's homes took over, carrying the baton until the late 1960s when children from schools in and around Wimbledon assumed responsibility. Until 1977 being a Wimbledon ball boy was strictly lads' stuff, girls making their debut that year (although it wasn't until 1986 that girls were allowed to work on the Centre Court). The selection process is tough and some might say pretty ruthless. Here's what tends to happen:

First, participating schools submit a list of their nominated boys and girls.

Although there are no weight or height restrictions all candidates must be physically fit, aged 14 or 15, available to start training at 4 p.m. after school and have no exams during the tournament.

All candidates have to pass a written test on the rules and scoring of tennis, plus other tests on hand-eye co-ordination. Fail, then it's the end of the road for the candidate.

All candidates have to show that they can stand still for three minutes and do speedy shuttle runs. Failure equals taxi for candidate.

Then, and only then, can a candidate qualify for full training. This begins in the February prior to each Wimbledon with ball boys and ball girls attending sessions at the National Tennis Centre in Roehampton and the Sutton Junior Tennis Centre in Surrey, though training switches to the All England Club from the Easter break onwards.

All candidates are constantly assessed throughout the training process on their general fitness, movement, ball skills (rolling, receiving, etc), scoring, set pieces (marching in line, what to do if play is suspended, etc). In the end around 250 lucky ones get chosen to take part in the Championships out of approximately 700 initial applicants. And they said building the Burma railway was tough . . .

The number of ball boys and girls used at Wimbledon has steadily increased over the years in line with the tournament's growth. Before the Second World War around 50 were required, a figure that had risen to approximately 140 by the early 1990s. Working in teams of six they spend one hour on court, one hour off court, the boy to girl ratio coming in at around 50/50. Being a Wimbledon ball boy/girl can be a rewarding experience but also a dangerous one. For every youngster hand-picked by a player to goof around in a rally on live TV, there's another who gets thwacked by a ball or, worse still, a player. How 15-year-old Erin Lorencin escaped serious injury in an accidental collision with Michael Llodra during Wimbledon 2009 still baffles me (Llodra was so beaten up he had to retire hurt). There's also the risk of public humiliation, slipping over while trying to retrieve a ball and having your misfortune posted on YouTube. All for absolutely no pocket money whatsoever!

WORKING CLASS

Wimbledon becomes something of a town within a town while the Championships are taking place. From souvenir shops and restaurants to banks and even a radio station (Radio Wimbledon, 87.7 FM), it's all there. As a result thousands of people converge on the All England Club during the tournament specifically to earn a living, many of them not the slightest bit interested in what happens on the courts. They include, in approximate numbers:

Catering staff (1,800)
Security guards (650)
Left luggage attendants (30)
Toilet attendants (112)
Office cleaners (75)
Ground cleaners (75)
Buildings maintenance personnel (85)
Courtesy drivers for officials, players, etc. (315)

Then there are those who work at Wimbledon either in a voluntary capacity or because their jobs are directly linked to the tennis, such as:

Players' dressing room attendants (22)
Groundsmen (20)
Match data collectors (36)

Honorary stewards (185)
Volunteer service stewards, such as firemen, soldiers on
    leave, etc (585)
Court attendants (140)
Umpires and line judges (340)
Physiotherapists (14)
Press Office staff (18)
Journalists and radio reporters (725)
Referee's Office (16)

THE SEEDING GAME

Every year in the days leading up to Wimbledon,
the All England Club unveils its lists of seeds for the
forthcoming tournament. What do these lists mean?
Well, the top seed will be the player deemed favourite
to win his or her event, the second seed the one most
likely to finish runner-up, and so on (the same principle
also applies to the Doubles competitions at Wimbledon
together with the Junior events). The main reason why
seeding takes place is to prevent the best players from
being drawn against each other during the early stages
of the tournament. Nobody wanted to see the likes of
Björn Borg versus John McEnroe in the first or second
rounds, so their seeding positions put them at opposite
ends of the draw where they were unlikely to meet until
the semi-finals or final. Seeding at the All England Club is
based roughly on world rankings. I say roughly because
Wimbledon, being Wimbledon, sometimes likes to put its
own little spin on the form book. For instance, in 2003
Tim Henman was seeded 10 even though he held a world

ranking of 29. The All England Club said it was because of his decent record on grass whereas the cynics argued it gave Henman a better chance of avoiding the danger men in the draw and making it through to the latter rounds. So how often does the All England Club get it right with its seeding predictions? Well it wasn't until 1995 that the top four seeds in both the Men and Women's Singles draws all made it through to the semi-finals. Here's a list of the number one male and female Wimbledon seeds between 1985 and 2000, and in brackets the name of the eventual winner each year:

Men
1985: John McEnroe (Boris Becker)
1986: Ivan Lendl (Boris Becker)
1987: Boris Becker (Pat Cash)
1988: Ivan Lendl (Stefan Edberg)
1989: Ivan Lendl (Boris Becker)
1990: Ivan Lendl (Stefan Edberg)
1991: Stefan Edberg (Michael Stich)
1992: Jim Courier (Andre Agassi)
1993: Pete Sampras (Pete Sampras)
1994: Pete Sampras (Pete Sampras)
1995: Andre Agassi (Pete Sampras)
1996: Pete Sampras (Richard Krajicek)
1997: Pete Sampras (Pete Sampras)
1998: Pete Sampras (Pete Sampras)
1999: Pete Sampras (Pete Sampras)
2000: Pete Sampras (Pete Sampras)

Women

1985: Chris Evert/Martina Navratilova jointly (Martina Navratilova)

1986: Martina Navratilova (Martina Navratilova)

1987: Martina Navratilova (Martina Navratilova)

1988: Steffi Graf (Steffi Graf)

1989: Steffi Graf (Steffi Graf)

1990: Steffi Graf (Martina Navratilova)

1991: Steffi Graf (Steffi Graf)

1992: Monica Seles (Steffi Graf)

1993: Steffi Graf (Steffi Graf)

1994: Steffi Graf (Conchita Martinez)

1995: Steffi Graf (Steffi Graf)

1996: Steffi Graf (Steffi Graf)

1997: Martina Hingis (Martina Hingis)

1998: Martina Hingis (Jana Novotna)

1999: Martina Hingis (Lindsay Davenport)

2000: Martina Hingis (Venus Williams)

SERVE & VOLLEY

Serve and volley is a term that describes a style of play which became especially popular in men's tennis during the 1980s and 1990s. With power all the rage thanks to super fit players using high-tech racquets, the idea of ramming down a serve and getting to the net to finish the point off as soon as possible became very much the norm. Spectators worldwide were divided about serve and volley. On the one hand they got to see some fireworks when it came to speeding-bullet serves and acrobatic smashes. On the other points tended to be over before you realised they had begun. In the 1991 Wimbledon Men's Singles final between Boris Becker and his German compatriot Michael Stich the average point lasted less than three measly seconds – not exactly edge-of-your-seat stuff. Come the twenty-first century serve and volley was beginning to die out and rallies were returning to major tennis events, helping to explain the extraordinary length of many Wimbledon Men's Singles finals in recent years.

ANDRE'S MIRACLE

Serve and volley was at its peak when Goran Ivanisevic and Andre Agassi went head to head in the Wimbledon Men's Singles final of 1992. Ivanisevic had arguably the fastest serve on the planet whereas Agassi was renowned as the world's best return of serve. Something had to give. Ivanisevic ended up hitting 37 aces – that works out at over nine games worth of aces – plus a shed load of other serves that were so powerful Agassi didn't have a prayer of getting them back. And yet Ivanisevic still lost. How did this happen? After Agassi had beaten John McEnroe in the semi-finals that year the magnanimous loser gave him a few tips on how best to deal with the sport's biggest servers. The advice boiled down to this – don't expect to get too many chances, make the most of the few that come your way, and refuse to let all the aces get you down. Agassi took McEnroe's words of wisdom and used them to his advantage against a stunned Ivanisevic, winning 6–7, 6–4, 6–4, 1–6, 6–4 in by far the most entertaining Men's Singles final since Jimmy Connors had overcome McEnroe in five dramatic sets in 1982.

THE GOSPEL ACCORDING TO GORAN

Goran Ivanisevic, as any sports writer will tell you, was always good for a quote. Here are a few of the Croatian's best spanning 2001, the year he won Wimbledon, through to his final Championships in 2004:

'If some angel comes tonight in my dreams and says, "Okay, Goran, you going to win Wimbledon tomorrow, but you not be able to touch the racquet ever again in your life," I say, "Okay, I rather take that and then never play tennis again."'

'God gave me another chance. He said, "Man, you were so annoying always asking for another chance . . . so, okay, I give you one more."'

'The trouble with me is that every match I play against five opponents; umpire, crowd, ball boys, court and myself.'

'Yes, I said that I would marry if I won Wimbledon, but this is a new century. New rules are valid now.'

'I still break racquets but now I do it in a positive way.'

'When I won Wimbledon I said to God, "Just let me win this one tournament and I won't play another match." Maybe God's telling me to go home, but I don't want to go home. We are negotiating at the moment.'

'If I can't serve on grass I can maybe help cut the grass, paint the lines and serve some strawberries.'

'I am going to miss everything about Wimbledon, the guys, serving aces on 15–40, talking to the umpire, watching the Teletubbies.'

'CAN WE ARM–WRESTLE?'

The longest match ever played at Wimbledon occurred during the 2006 Championships and involved a Men's Doubles quarter-final between Mark Knowles and Daniel Nestor and Simon Aspelin and Todd Perry. The tie began on the Wednesday of the second week and finished the following day after 6 hours and 9 minutes play. Knowles and Nestor were the eventual winners having saved six match points against them in the fifth set, the final score being 5–7, 6–3, 6–7, 6–3, 23–21. 'It got to the point where you're thinking "Can we arm-wrestle or do something else just to end this?"' said Knowles afterwards, an equally fatigued Nestor admitting that, 'It definitely wasn't humorous for me. At times I was wondering if it was ever going to end.' Play had been suspended on the Wednesday evening at 11–11 in the final set which alone lasted over 3 hours. The record was previously held by Greg Holmes and Todd Witsken who took 5 hours 28 minutes to complete their second-round match in the Men's Singles in 1989.

THE MATCH THAT HAD EVERYTHING

For anyone old enough to remember it one titanic Wimbledon match in particular stands head and shoulders above the others. In 1969 the 5 hours and 12 minutes that Pancho Gonzales needed to beat Charlie Pasarell by 22–24, 1–6, 16–14, 6–3, 11–9 set a new Championship record. But the scoreline tells only half the story. For a start Gonzales, 41 at the time, had previously coached Pasarell who was 16 years his junior. The match would have been even longer had Gonzales not thrown a hissy-fit and deliberately chucked the second set because umpire Harold Duncombe initially refused to suspend play due to bad light. When the pair resumed hostilities the following day Gonzales was two sets down and in a hole, the crowd having turned against him the night before. This time around the spectators, keen to see more action, warmed to his attempts to get back into the match. Gonzales clinched the 30-game third set when Pasarell hit two double faults, then cruised through the fourth to take the tie into a deciding fifth. By the end both players were physically wiped out, Gonzales fending off seven match points against him and twice recovering from 0–40 to book his place in the second round. The fact that chairs didn't exist then for players to sit on during changes of ends only adds another dimension to their exhaustion. For the record Gonzales recovered to win his next two Singles matches before running into Arthur Ashe in the fourth round. It was feared by many tennis followers – wrongly, as it turned out – that the introduction of tie-breaks at Wimbledon in 1971 would kill-off such epic battles as Gonzales versus Pasarell.

FAMILY AFFAIR

The competitive streak that exists within some families means that many brothers and sisters have turned up at Wimbledon as rivals. Take the Watson sisters for example, Maud and Lilian, who faced one another in the first ever Women's Singles final back in 1884. Then there were the Renshaw brothers, William and Ernest, who went head to head three times at the All England Club in 1882, 1883 and 1889 (William winning each time). However, two families have taken this sibling rivalry stuff to extremes. In 1977 no less than three brothers – Tony, David and John Lloyd – took part in the Men's Singles competition though the draw mercifully kept them apart. During the early 1990s the trio of Maleeva sisters – Manuela, Katerina and Magdalena – all competed in the Women's Singles on three separate occasions, each one of them being seeded at the 1993 Championships.

MR AND MRS

They say the chances of meeting your future spouse at work are extremely high, which probably explains why 13 married couples took part in the Wimbledon Mixed Doubles event in 1968.

MUM'S THE WORD

In 1931 and 1932 Raymond Tuckey made headlines by playing in the Mixed Doubles event at Wimbledon alongside his dear old mum, Agnes, who had won the competition twice in her prime at the 1909 and 1913 Championships. They reached the third round in 1931 but were knocked out at the first hurdle 12 months later. During the 1932 tournament Agnes was just a few days short of her fifty-fifth birthday making her Wimbledon's oldest ever competitor (excluding Veterans' events) at that time.

SISTER SLUDGE

Unquestionably the most famous family double act around Wimbledon of recent times has been the Williams sisters. Initially it was Venus who dominated, winning the Women's Singles finals of 2000 and 2001. Then Serena showed up, beating her sister in the 2002 and 2003 finals before losing to Maria Sharapova in 2004. In 2005 Venus reclaimed the Wimbledon crown, going on to win the finals of 2007 and 2008 (the latter versus her sister) before falling to Serena at the last hurdle in 2009. However, more often than not matches between the pair have been strangely flat affairs. For years rumours abounded that whenever the sisters met, dad Richard would call the shots in advance over which one should prevail. In reality the truth is probably something far less sinister – Venus and Serena just don't like playing against each another, finding the whole process an ordeal which dampens their competitive juices. To make matters worse for the rest of the female field the sisters traditionally join forces in the Women's Doubles at Wimbledon, treating the event as extra training for the Singles on their way to the 2000, 2002, 2008 and 2009 titles.

COMEBACK KING

It's probably just as well that Jimmy Connors didn't have a professional tennis playing brother. You see Connors was one of those rare competitors who simply never gave up. In other words Connors versus Connors would have been a match played until the end of time. One of the great fightbacks of his long career came in the fourth round at Wimbledon in 1987. Connors was 34 and without a Grand Slam title in four years. Age, it seemed, was finally catching up with one of the sport's all-time greats. His opponent that day was the Swedish player Mikael Pernfors, unseeded but still a dangerous presence in the draw. Pernfors comfortably won the first two sets, both 6–1, before establishing a 4–1 lead in the third against a strangely subdued Connors who was nursing a slight leg injury. Talk about anti-climatic for the Centre Court crowd who had gathered to cheer on the veteran American. Then, with the match almost up, the tide suddenly turned. Connors began hitting winners, his trademark fist-pumping celebrations coming thick and fast. He won the third set 7–5, then set about dismantling the startled Pernfors whose mind was already in the changing room celebrating a comfortable straight sets victory. All told, Connors won 18 of the last 25 games taking the fourth and fifth sets 6–4 and 6–2 respectively. 'My ego was hurt,' said Connors afterwards. 'I had to do something, so I decided to fight even harder.'

BORG'S LET OFF

Björn Borg was so dominant around Wimbledon during the mid-to-late 1970s and early '80s that it's easy to forget the handful of genuine occasions when he came close to losing. Perhaps his closest brush with defeat during that epic run of five consecutive Singles titles spanning 1976 to 1980 was against the late Vitas Gerulaitis in the 1977 semi-finals. Borg and Gerulaitis were friends and training partners who knew each other's games inside out. The match see-sawed over the course of the first four sets; 6–4 Borg, 6–3 Gerulaitis, 6–3 Borg, 6–3 Gerulaitis. So it continued deep into the fifth when, in the gathering Centre Court gloom, Gerulaitis reached match point. Faced with a relatively straight forward backhand down the line the underdog was suddenly caught in two minds about how to play the shot. Instead of going for power, Gerulaitis went for slice . . . and the ball floated long. Borg made the most of his reprieve going on to take that deciding set 8–6. Gerulaitis – who died of carbon monoxide poisoning through a faulty propane heater in 1994 – reached three Grand Slam finals during a colourful career, winning one, but it is for this particular match that he is probably best remembered.

LARISA'S LONGEST DAY

Another rainy tale I'm afraid. Well, what do you expect? This is a book about Wimbledon! The second week of the 1996 Championships was severely affected by bad weather. The All England Club attempted to deal with the growing backlog of matches by starting play at 11 a.m. from Tuesday onwards, but it still wasn't enough. Come the Sunday three events – the Women's Doubles, the Mixed Doubles and the Girls' Doubles – still hadn't finished, so the decision was made to extend the Championships to a third Monday. On that day over 13,000 spectators were admitted free of charge to watch the remaining matches, four of which featured Larisa Neiland of Latvia. You've got to feel for poor Neiland. It is every player's dream to appear on the Centre Court but competing in four matches in a row there spanning a grand total of 6 hours 25 minutes must have been exhausting, not to mention surreal. To make matters worse she lost in both the Women's and the Mixed Doubles finals.

TWO OUT OF THREE AIN'T BAD

Louise Brough endured a similar experience to Larisa Neiland when she competed at Wimbledon in 1949, taking part in three matches on the last day of the Championships consisting of a mammoth 117 games. This time, however, the outcome was a slightly happier one, Brough winning both the Women's Singles final and the Doubles while having to make do with a runner-up salver in the Mixed. In an ironic twist the player Brough defeated in the Women's final, Margaret du Pont, was also her partner in the Women's Doubles.

'LITTLE MO'

No book on Wimbledon would be complete without a few words about Maureen Connolly, better known to millions simply as 'Little Mo'. Born in San Diego in 1934, Connolly took up tennis as a child because her parents were unable to afford the horse she so desperately wanted. By the time she turned 20 Connolly had won the Wimbledon Singles title three times (in 1952, 1953 and 1954). Why the 'Little Mo' nickname? That was the work of American sports writers who compared her explosive style of play to the battleship USS *Missouri*, known as 'Big Mo', which was based in San Diego. Just days after beating Louise Brough in the 1954 final, Connolly broke her right leg in a riding accident. The injury was so severe that 'Little Mo' announced her retirement in February 1955, aware she would struggle to recapture her devastating form of old. Connolly – unbeaten in Singles at Wimbledon – never lost her love of horses or the sport that had made her famous, going on to start a foundation aimed at encouraging children to take up tennis. Tragically she died of stomach cancer in 1969 at the ridiculously young age of 34. 'Whenever a great player comes along you have to ask, "Could she have beaten Maureen?" and in every case the answer is I think not,' wrote the *Daily Telegraph's* long-standing tennis correspondent Lance Tingay of one of the sport's true greats.

WHEELCHAIR WIMBLEDON

Being confined to a wheelchair doesn't mean you can't play tennis. Far from it. Over the past few years wheelchair tennis has exploded onto the scene with players from all over the world taking part in tournaments including Grand Slam events. Wheelchair tennis made its competitive debut at Wimbledon during the 2005 Championships when four pairs took part in a Men's Doubles event. However, the first wheelchair match at the All England Club was actually a demonstration of the sport involving four British players held during the 2001 tournament. Yorkshireman Kevin Plowman, paralysed from the chest down in a mountaineering accident when he was 28, served the first ball (the BBC recorded the action and screened it that afternoon during a rain-enforced break in play). 'That was my finest day,' Kevin admitted a few years later. 'I became the first wheelchair player ever to hit a ball at Wimbledon. Afterwards my girlfriend and I went to watch a bit of Tim Henman's semi-final against Goran Ivanisevic and we couldn't move for people asking to have their picture taken with me and sign their programmes. It was my five minutes of fame. I loved it.'

NO JOKE

Heard the one about the Irish tennis player? In 1889 Lena Rice came to Wimbledon from the village of New Inn, Tipperary, and lost to Blanche Hillyard. Twelve months later Rice returned and became the Women's Singles Champion. Okay, so only four ladies entered that year but she still goes down in the history books as a Wimbledon winner alongside the likes of Martina Navratilova and the Williams sisters. Oh yeah, there's something else you should know about Lena Rice. She was born in New Inn on 21 June 1866 and died in New Inn on 21 June 1907. Not much of a forty-first birthday then for Lena.

THE UPS AND DOWNS OF WIMBLEDON

'I was seven years old and my hero was Andre Agassi. I really wanted his autograph but I couldn't get near him.'
Andy Murray remembers his first visit to Wimbledon

'They should send Borg away to another planet. We play tennis. He plays something else.'
Ilie Nastase after losing the 1976 Wimbledon Men's Singles final to Björn Borg

'I'll chase that son of a bitch Borg to the ends of the earth. I'll be waiting for him. I'll dog him everywhere. Every time he looks around he'll see my shadow.'
Jimmy Connors on his Wimbledon nemesis Björn Borg

'Until I win or die.'
Ivan Lendl on how long he would keep trying to win Wimbledon

'There's a really long tunnel from the dressing room to Court One, it's about a five-minute walk, and when I got to the end I wanted to turn back, but I couldn't, partly because Sampras was right behind me.'
Barry Cowan battles nerves ahead of his 2001 clash with Pete Sampras

'I've always had this little thing I do when I tie my shoes. I finish tying them, slap the ground and say to myself "Here we go!" But this time it didn't feel good. And I stopped, right there and then.'

Pete Sampras withdraws from Wimbledon, 2003, and retires from tennis

'I went in on his forehand and he passed me. I went in on his backhand and he passed me. I stayed back and he passed me even though I was at the baseline.'

Andy Roddick after losing to Roger Federer in the 2005 Wimbledon Men's Singles final

'Maybe I'll just punch him or something.'

Andy Roddick, again, after the same match

'I had always dreamed of winning Wimbledon and when it happened it was very stressful. It was more of a relief!'

Pat Cash on winning Wimbledon in 1987

'It definitely hurts less to lose to her. I mean, I'll be bitter, but at the end of the day it's a lot easier to losing to someone that I feel I should normally beat.'

Serena Williams ahead of one of her many Wimbledon showdowns with sister Venus

'Nobody can tell me to stop grunting. If they have to fine me, go ahead, 'cause I'd rather get fined than lose a match because I had to stop grunting. If people don't like my grunting they can always leave.'

Chief 'grunter' Michelle Larcher de Brito hits back at her Wimbledon critics, 2009

INSTANT REPLAY

The 1902 Wimbledon Women's Singles final brought together defending Champion Charlotte Sterry of Middlesex and Northumberland's Muriel Robb, making her one and only appearance in the last two. Robb began well in overcast conditions taking the first set 6–4. The second seemed to go on forever until Sterry eventually levelled the scores by taking it 13–11, at which point the heavens opened forcing the players off court for the rest of the day. When the players reconvened at Worple Road the next morning some bright spark decided it would be a good idea if the match started all over again. And that's exactly what happened. The slate was wiped clean and Robb went on to claim the title with a 7–5, 6–1 win making it the longest Women's Singles final ever at 53 games, providing you take into account the two abandoned sets.

SELLING ENGLAND BY THE POUND

In 1923 the All England Club sold their grounds at Worple Road to the Wimbledon High School for Girls, which still owns the site today. The school paid £4,000 for the land.

DEVON 1 ESSEX 0

It was the first time it had happened since 1914 and, going by the evidence of today, it'll be the last time it happens until you and I are long, long gone. In 1961 two British players went head to head at Wimbledon in the Women's Singles final when Plymouth-born Angela Mortimer took on Essex girl Christine Truman. It proved to be a cracking encounter as Mortimer fought back from a set down to take the title with a 4–6, 6–4, 7–5 victory, consolation of sorts for the Devonian's defeat to Althea Gibson in the 1958 final.

MAX FACTOR

In 1921 Liverpool-born Max Woosnam won the Wimbledon Men's Doubles competition along with Randolph Lycett. Not bad when you consider Woosnam was better known for his exploits with balls of a slightly larger nature, playing centre-half for Chelsea and Manchester City as well as earning a solitary England cap in 1922.

THE MATTHEWS FINAL

In 1962 Stanley Matthews won Junior Wimbledon. No, really! Oh alright, it wasn't actually the famous England footballer but his son, also called Stanley, who defeated the Georgian youngster Alexander Metreveli 10–8, 3–6, 6–4 in the final.

SECURITY GLASS

Goalkeeper Jimmy Glass was a strictly second-division footballer compared to Stanley Matthews. However, that didn't prevent him from making headlines around the world in 1999, scoring a dramatic goal in the final minute of the final game of the season to keep struggling Carlisle United in the Football League (they stayed up and Scarborough went into the non-league abyss, all because of Jimmy's 95th-minute strike). While learning his goalkeeping trade at Crystal Palace, Glass actually moonlighted as a security guard at Wimbledon during the 1992 Championships. He spent most of the fortnight working as a 'Player Escort', protecting competitors from any unwanted attention that might come their way. The highlight of his security stint came when he was chosen to walk Gabriela Sabatini back to her rented accommodation, the pair exchanging some brief chit-chat along the way about football (Sabatini supports the Argentinian side River Plate).

THE UNDERDOG

Wimbledon loves an underdog. True, complete unknowns don't tend to win the tournament but quite a few have come tantalisingly close to the ultimate prize. See how many of the following you remember:

Chris Lewis
New Zealander Lewis, complete with his fetching bandana, came out of nowhere to reach the 1983 Men's Singles final

where he was blown away in straight sets by John McEnroe. He played the match of his life in the semi-finals, edging out Kevin Curren 8–6 in the fifth set.

MaliVai Washington
The unseeded American reached the Men's Singles final in 1996 only to run out of steam against Richard Krajicek. Like Lewis, he also survived an epic semi, overcoming Todd Martin 10–8 in a fifth set.

Cedric Pioline
Frenchman Pioline saw off both Greg Rusedski and Michael Stich on his way to the 1997 Men's Singles final before being ruthlessly dispatched by Pete Sampras.

Marion Bartoli
Also from France, Bartoli had never progressed beyond the third round at Wimbledon prior to making the Women's Singles final in 2007. Her day in the sun against Venus Williams turned out to be rabbit in car headlights stuff, the all-conquering American winning 6–4, 6–1.

Mark Philippoussis
Not strictly an unknown but the Australian did reach the last two in 2003 as an unseeded player where he became Roger Federer's first Men's Singles final victim.

Zheng Jie
Not a finalist but did become the first Chinese player ever to reach a Grand Slam Singles semi when she took on Serena Williams in 2008. Didn't do too badly either, losing with honours 6–2, 7–6. Also had the consolation

of being the first wildcard player ever to reach the semis of the Women's Singles at Wimbledon.

Slobodan Zivojinovic

The giant Yugoslavian with the vicious serve and the unpronounceable name made an indelible mark on the 1986 Championships, reaching the semi-finals as an unseeded player before losing in five closely contested sets to Ivan Lendl.

Henri Leconte

Like Philippoussis, not strictly an unknown, yet still something of an underdog. Leconte never won a Grand Slam title but was always a popular draw with the Wimbledon crowds, reaching the semi-finals in 1986 where he lost to Boris Becker.

Boris Becker

Sure, you've heard of him now. But, let's face it, how many people knew Becker's name when he played his first-round Singles match against Hank Pfister in 1985?

STAMP OF APPROVAL

It goes without saying that winning Wimbledon opens all kinds of doors for a tennis player. It can also result in a blizzard of other bizarre spin-offs such as being presented with a cow (Roger Federer – see 'Juliette Bravo'), having a ticker tape parade thrown in your honour (Maria Bueno) or getting compared to Jesus Christ (Goran Ivanisevic, as according to Croatian legend 'only Goran and Jesus have been resurrected'). Several champions have been immortalised in wax by Madame Tussauds while others glory in public holidays declared in their names as a mark of respect. Win Wimbledon and you can expect to see your head on a postage stamp (Federer in Switzerland, Rod Laver in Australia, Boris Becker in, er, Paraguay) and your doormat swamped with invitations to wine and dine with celebrities, politicians or even royalty. Alternatively you could end up with a Grand Slam tennis court named after you (Arthur Ashe at Flushing Meadows, Margaret Court in Melbourne Park, Suzanne Lenglen at Roland Garros). In fact Wimbledon is the only Grand Slam tennis venue without a court named after a former player.

ARTHUR'S INFLUENCE

Arthur Ashe wasn't the first black person ever to win a Wimbledon title. However, the waves sent out by his 1975 Men's Singles final victory over Jimmy Connors were to change the face of tennis forever. Born in 1943, Ashe grew up the son of a policeman in Richmond, Virginia. He regarded tennis as a passport to better things, his rise to the top becoming something of a crusade on behalf of underprivileged, downtrodden people everywhere. Ashe ruled in a white man's world where antiquated attitudes to race were dying hard. Sure, he was on the receiving end of some vitriolic attacks from extremists, yet Ashe never seemed to let it bother him, preferring instead to let his racquet do the talking. When he did speak out he refused to become a militant mouthpiece, talking eloquently in public about civil rights. Ashe wasn't expected to beat

Connors. Age was against him (he was a week away from turning 32) and defending Champion Connors, besides being top seed, had been in ruthless form for months. Somehow the 'veteran' turned the formbook on its head to win 6–1, 6–1, 5–7, 6–4 (he remains the oldest Men's Wimbledon Champion of the post-1968 Open era). Ashe already had two Grand Slam titles under his belt but the fact this was Wimbledon, widely regarded as the 'stuffiest' event of them all, made one hell of an impression. Thanks to Ashe, non-white kids from Los Angeles to Lagos began picking up tennis racquets, some going on to earn a healthy living from the sport. One of them, Yannick Noah, even partnered Ashe at Wimbledon in 1978, forming the first black Doubles team ever seen at the All England Club. 'The way I see things, what I do, the way I behave, he's really a part of me,' said Noah shortly after Ashe's premature death in 1993 of an AIDS-related illness (Ashe had contracted HIV from a blood transfusion in 1983). 'Him having the same colour as me, he was my hero.'

THE KENTS

Like so many other Wimbledon Champions, Arthur Ashe received his trophy from the Duke of Kent, President of the All England Club. The duke presented his first trophy way back in 1969 to Rod Laver, winner of the Men's Singles final. For many years it was the norm for him to present the men with their trophies and his wife, the Duchess of Kent, to do likewise with the women. However, since 2003 the duke has presented the lion's share of the trophies to the winners of all competitions owing to the duchess' absence through ill-health. Occasionally the Kents have taken a back seat allowing someone else to do the honours. This select list includes Her Majesty Queen Elizabeth II who handed the Rosewater Dish to Virginia Wade in 1977, together with former Wimbledon greats Jean Borotra and Kathleen 'Kitty' Godfree who presented Boris Becker and Martina Navratilova with their respective trophies in 1986. Since 1954 all presentation ceremonies involving Singles Champions and runners-up have taken place on the Centre Court turf itself, with Doubles and Junior finalists being honoured in the Royal Box.

COIN-TOSSERS

If the presentation of trophies marks the end of a Wimbledon final then the toss of a coin represents the beginning. The official 'Coin Tossing Ceremony' is a relatively new Wimbledon tradition dating back to 2000. It involves two people – usually children or teenagers – tossing a coin before the respective Singles finals to see which player serves first. The lucky pair are chosen by charities or organisations nominated in turn by people well connected with Wimbledon. For instance, in 2000 a 12-year-old boy called Raju Tital tossed the coin ahead of the Women's Singles final between Lindsay Davenport and Venus Williams. Raju, an orphan found the previous year in poor health at a Calcutta railway station, was selected by a charity supported by the Duchess of Kent called Future Hope. Appropriately the coin tossed on that occasion was an Indian one rupee piece dating back to the 1830s. Not all the coin-tossers are youngsters, though. In 2005 top British wheelchair player Peter Norfolk was on duty for the Men's Singles final between Roger Federer and Andy Roddick.

EVERYBODY OUT!

Tennis was blessed with some unbelievable talents during the 1960s and early '70s. Unfortunately the paying public were often denied the opportunity of watching their favourite players in action due to various disputes which affected tennis as a whole rather than just Wimbledon. The longest running of these was the whole amateur versus professional soap opera which saw professional players banned from appearing at amateur Grand Slam events up until 1968, the year tennis finally became 'Open' to all. However, that didn't prevent another situation from flaring up in 1972 when a ridiculous spat between the International Lawn Tennis Federation and World Championship Tennis saw the ILTF ban a number of players with professional contracts from appearing at some tournaments. As a result the reigning Wimbledon Champion John Newcombe, one of the most popular players on the circuit, lost the chance to defend his title. Worse was to come the following year when 79 players – all men – boycotted Wimbledon in protest at the ILTF's suspension of the Yugoslavian player Nikki Pilic (Pilic had been suspended by his national association for not playing in a Davis Cup tie, the ILTF backing the decision). The newly formed Association of Tennis Professionals

(ATP), born partly out of frustration over the autocratic behaviour of various national associations, urged players to take a stand – and take a stand vast numbers of them did by not showing up in SW19. The real loser in what amounted to a 'Who runs what?' squabble between the ILTF and the ATP was the public. Mind you, there was one man who ended up benefitting big time from the whole farce . . .

JAN THE MAN

Jan Kodes was a decent enough tennis player but there is no way he would have come within a sniff of winning Wimbledon in any year other than 1973. With 79 players missing from the Men's draw due to the boycott, including 13 of the 16 seeds, those who remained suddenly realised they had a once in a lifetime opportunity to scoop the jackpot. Prague-born Kodes, then 27, had won the French Open in both 1970 and 1971 but his form at Wimbledon was wretched with five first-round Singles defeats on his CV. This time Kodes was able to go the whole way through a field consisting largely of unknown qualifiers, breaking British hearts in the semi-finals with a five-set win over Sheffield's Roger Taylor. In the final he defeated Alexander Metreveli 6–1, 9–8, 6–3 to become one of the unlikeliest Wimbledon Champions ever.

FINAL COUNTDOWN

Some Wimbledon finals are forgotten within hours of the Championships ending. Others live in the memory for years to come. Here's a list of 10 of the best:

Rafael Nadal v Roger Federer (2008)
Arguably the finest tennis match ever played on Planet Earth. Nadal won in five, 6–4, 6–4, 6–7, 6–7, 9–7.

Roger Federer v Andy Roddick (2009)
Roddick played the match of his life and it still wasn't enough, Federer triumphing 5–7, 7–5, 7–6, 3–6, 16–14.

John McEnroe v Björn Borg (1980)
Borg won his fifth and final Wimbledon 1–6, 7–5, 6–3, 6–7, 8–6 in a match featuring *that* never to be forgotten 34-point tie break.

Andre Agassi v Goran Ivanisevic (1992)
At times this was more like watching a sniper taking pot shots at a poodle, such was the awesome power of the 37-ace Ivanisevic serve. And yet somehow the poodle stood its ground to win 6–7, 6–4, 6–4, 1–6, 6–4.

Jimmy Connors v John McEnroe (1982)
A match given added spice by the two finalists clearly not being on each other's Christmas card lists, Connors winning a second Wimbledon Singles title eight years after his first.

Goran Ivanisevic v Pat Rafter (2001)

Wildcard Ivanisevic finally came good in his fourth Wimbledon Singles final, one of the more emotional (and unlikely) ever witnessed on the Centre Court.

Margaret Court v Billie Jean King (1970)

Both players were carrying injuries, not that you would have guessed judging by the power and passion of their play. Court won 14–12, 11–9 in what at the time was the longest Women's Singles final ever.

Suzanne Lenglen v Dorothea Lambert Chambers (1919)

Lenglen won the first of her six Wimbledon Singles titles in what ranks as the greatest final ever played at the old Worple Road grounds, defeating Chambers (who was 20 years her senior) 10–8, 4–6, 9–7.

Venus Williams v Lindsay Davenport (2005)

Davenport, struggling with a back strain, served for the match at 6–5 in the second set and had a match point in the third, yet Williams prevailed 4–6, 7–6, 9–7 in the longest Women's Singles final on record (2 hours and 46 minutes).

Arthur Ashe v Jimmy Connors (1975)

A triumph of tactics and experience over brute strength and youth as Ashe varied the pace and power of his shots to throw the younger Connors completely off his stride, winning 6–1, 6–1, 5–7, 6–4.

SEEING DOUBLE

It is a fact of Wimbledon life that the Doubles tends to take a back seat compared to the glitz of the Singles competitions. There are, however, some people who love nothing more than going to Wimbledon and finding an obscure Doubles match on an outside court to get completely absorbed in. And who can blame them judging by some of the quality pairs who have strutted their stuff at the All England Club down the years, duos such as John Newcombe and Tony Roche, Ken Rosewall and Fred Stolle, Peter McNamara and Paul McNamee, Tim and Tom Gullikson, Martina Navratilova and Pam Shriver, Peter Fleming and John McEnroe, the Bryan brothers, and so on. During the 1990s one pair in particular came to be synonymous with the doubles game. Both were pretty handy singles players in their own right, yet in the team game grew to be virtually unbeatable. They were Todd Woodbridge and Mark Woodforde, the Australians who won the Men's Doubles competition at Wimbledon in 1993, 1994, 1995, 1996 and 1997. In 1998, shock horror, 'The Woodies' were actually beaten in the final but bounced back to win the event again in 2000 shortly before Woodforde retired. As if that wasn't enough, Woodbridge then paired up with the Swedish player Jonas Björkman to win the Men's Doubles event again in 2002, 2003 and 2004 before himself retiring in 2005. But wait, there's more. Woodbridge and Woodforde also won the Mixed Doubles event. No, not together, but alongside Helena Sukova (in 1994) and Martina Navratilova (1993) respectively.

ACES HIGH

Before tennis racquets became all high-tech and players morphed into pumped up uber-beings the serve was regarded by the majority of competitors as just another shot. Then in the 1970s along came Roscoe Tanner who word had it actually practised his serving by firing balls at empty drinks cans, hitting them at around 100 miles per hour. The bar had been raised and with new metal and graphite racquet designs on the market the serve quickly became a weapon. The introduction of radar guns at tournaments measuring speed of service has led to healthy competition within dressing rooms as players go all-out to see who can hit the fastest (the 'gun' was first used on the Centre Court in 1991 and on Court 1 six years later). At the time of writing the owner of Wimbledon's fastest serve is Andy Roddick (146mph, 2004) while Venus Williams was timed at 129mph during the 2008 Championships, a record for the women.

FRENCH CONNECTION

Despite its reputation for being a clay court nation, France has enjoyed a visible presence around Wimbledon over recent years with Amelie Mauresmo winning the Women's Singles final in 2006 and Cedric Pioline, Nathalie Tauziat and Marion Bartoli all finishing as runners-up in 1997, 1998 and 2007 respectively. That's still small fry compared to the French glory years of the 1920s when the 'Four Musketeers' – Jean Borotra, Jacques Brugnon, Henri Cochet and René Lacoste – dominated the Men's

Singles and Doubles at Wimbledon. Borotra, Cochet and Lacoste each triumphed in the Singles twice (all three also finished as runners-up) while the quartet shared five Men's Doubles titles between them. Throw in Suzanne Lenglen's stunning achievements in the Women's Singles from 1919 to 1925 (she won it six times) and you can see why the French always wore such wide grins around SW19.

TROUSER PRESS

There has only been one French Men's Singles Champion at Wimbledon since the Second World War. His name was Yvon Petra and he won the title in 1946 defeating the Australian Geoffrey Brown. In doing so Petra ensured newspaper mentions for decades to come by being the last man to win Wimbledon while playing in trousers.

QUEEN MARTINA EQUALS KING'S RECORD

Petra's 1946 Men's Singles final victory proved to be the only Wimbledon title of the Frenchman's career. Compare that with Martina Navratilova who in 2003 finally equalled Billie Jean King's record of 20 Championship titles. It came in the Mixed Doubles competition, Navratilova partnering Leander Paes to a 6–3, 6–3 win over Andy Ram and Anastasia Rodionova in the final. At the time she was three months shy of her 47th birthday, Navratilova shedding a few uncharacteristic tears on court after Paes had hit the winning smash. A couple of days beforehand she had become the first player of either gender to appear in 300 matches at Wimbledon. Will we see her like again? It's doubtful, especially with so few of the top Singles players now appearing in the Doubles competitions. No wonder Paes did an 'I'm not worthy' bow in her direction having just clinched victory.

MAC'S FINAL BOW

John McEnroe was another player who took his doubles duties seriously, never more so than at the 1992 Wimbledon Championships. Towards the end of the second week the fine weather which had blessed the tournament broke big time resulting in the Friday being completely washed out. As a result Wimbledon was extended to a third Monday so several matches could be completed, one of them being the Men's Doubles final between McEnroe and Michael Stich and Jim Grabb and Richey Reneberg. The match had begun on the Sunday but with both pairs digging in for the long haul it was held over until the following day. Around 8,000 spectators turned up on the Monday to watch whatever action they could, drawn by the offer of free admission plus the chance of seeing McEnroe, not to mention former Wimbledon winner Stich, in action. They wouldn't be disappointed as the match proved to be a classic, McEnroe and Stich prevailing 5–7, 7–6, 3–6, 7–6, 19–17 after 301 minutes in what proved to be the former's last competitive match at the All England Club.

BEST OF THE BEST

So which players have won the most Singles titles at Wimbledon throughout the years? Here's a list of the All England Club's best of the best:

Men

7 – William Renshaw (1881–6, 1889)

7 – Pete Sampras (1993–5, 1997–2000)

6 – Roger Federer (2003–7, 2009)

5 – Hugh Doherty (1902–6)

5 – Björn Borg (1976–80)

4 – Reginald Doherty (1897–1900)

4 – Anthony Wilding (1910–13)

4 – Rod Laver (1961/2, 1968/9)

3 – Wilfred Baddeley (1891/92, 1895)

3 – Arthur Gore (1901, 1908/9)

3 – William Tilden (1920/1, 1930)

3 – Fred Perry (1934–6)

3 – John Newcombe (1967, 1970/1)

3 – John McEnroe (1981, 1983/4)

3 – Boris Becker (1985/6, 1989)

Women

9 – Martina Navratilova (1978/9, 1982–7, 1990)

8 – Helen Wills/Mrs F.S. Moody (1927–30, 1932/3, 1935, 1938)

7 – Dorothea Douglass/Mrs R.L. Chambers (1903/4, 1906, 1910/11, 1913/14)

7 – Steffi Graf (1988/9, 1991–3, 1995/6)

6 – Blanche Bingley/Mrs G. Hillyard (1886, 1889, 1894, 1897, 1899/1900)

6 – Suzanne Lenglen (1919–23, 1925)
6 – Billie Jean King (1966–8, 1972/3, 1975)
5 – Charlotte 'Lottie' Dod (1887/8, 1891–3)
5 – Charlotte Cooper/Mrs A. Sterry (1895/6, 1898,
   1901, 1908)
5 – Venus Williams (2000/1, 2005, 2007/8)
4 – Louise Brough (1948–50, 1955)
3 – Maria Bueno (1959/60, 1964)
3 – Maureen Connolly (1952–4)
3 – Margaret Smith/Mrs B.M. Court (1963, 1965, 1970)
3 – Chris Evert/Mrs J.M. Lloyd (1974, 1976, 1981)
3 – Serena Williams (2002/3, 2009)

LEST WE FORGET

A few lines about Anthony Wilding, or rather Tony Wilding as he was more commonly known, winner of four consecutive Wimbledon Men's Singles titles from 1910 to 1913. Wilding was born in Christchurch, New Zealand, in 1883. He came to England at the age of 19 to study at Cambridge where he played on the university's tennis team. By 1905 he was a member of the Australasian Davis Cup side, qualifying as a barrister four years later back home in New Zealand. Wilding finally won Wimbledon in 1910 at his sixth attempt, defeating Arthur Gore in the final. He wouldn't lose another match at the All England Club until the final of 1914 when he was unseated by Australia's Norman Brookes in straight sets. On the outbreak of the First World War just weeks later, Wilding joined the Royal Marines serving as a captain in France. He was killed in action at the age of 31 on 9 May 1915 at Neuve Chapelle, his final resting place being the Rue-des-Berceaux Military Cemetery in the village of Richebourg-L'Avoue, Pas de Calais. Wilding Park, the main tennis centre in Christchurch, is named in his memory. Fine scholar, great tennis player, good sportsman, avid motorbike enthusiast . . . no wonder Wilding is still fondly remembered around the world.

OLYMPIC SPIRIT

London's successful bid to stage the 2012 Olympic Games meant SW19 was a natural venue for the tennis events. The last time Wimbledon hosted Olympic tennis was in 1908 when the All England Club was based at Worple Road rather than its present day home at Church Road. Back then Britain still ruled the world at tennis. As a result UK players won all bar one of the medals in every event (the Men's Singles, Women's Singles and Men's Doubles, the ladies going without a pairs competition), the exception being the silver medal in the Men's Singles which went to the German Otto Froitzheim who was beaten by Josiah Ritchie in the final. By the time the Games returned to London in 1948 tennis had severed its links with the Olympic movement, pulling the plug after Paris in 1924. It returned in a demonstration capacity at the 1968 and 1984 Olympics in Mexico City and Los Angeles respectively, before once again becoming an official medal sport at Seoul in 1988. Whether tennis should in fact be an Olympic sport considering the vast wealth in the upper echelons of the game remains something of a moot point.

CLEAN SWEEP

It takes something to win the hat-trick at Wimbledon. By hat-trick I mean the Singles, Doubles and Mixed Doubles. The first player to achieve a clean sweep was the indomitable Suzanne Lenglen of France who won the Women's Singles, Women's Doubles and Mixed Doubles competitions in 1920, 1922 and 1925. Twelve years later John 'Don' Budge won the Men's Singles, Men's Doubles and Mixed Doubles, repeating the feat in 1938. Since then six other players have added their names to the roll of honour. They are Bobby Riggs (1939), Alice Marble (1939), Louise Brough (1948 and 1950), Doris Hart (1951), Frank Sedgman (1952) and Billie Jean King (1967 and 1973). Today the top players, concerned about spreading themselves too thinly, are understandably reluctant to enter three competitions meaning hat-tricks are unlikely ever to be seen at Wimbledon again.

ONCE, TWICE, THREE TIMES A LOSER

There is of course a flip side to the scenario of winning a hat-trick of titles at Wimbledon in the same year, and that is finishing runner-up in three events. Five players have endured this miserable experience, among them Doris Hart – the heroine of 1951 – who three years previously finished second best in the Women's Singles, Women's Doubles and Mixed Doubles. The other poor unfortunates are Howard Kinsey (1926), Geoffrey Brown (1946), Margaret Court (1971) and Betty Stöve (1977) who lost her Singles final to Britain's Virginia Wade.

AMERICAN IDOLS

To say America's ladies were in menacing form when Wimbledon resumed in 1946 following a six-year, war-enforced hiatus would be a huge understatement. Get this – the next 10 Women's Singles finals up to and including 1955 all involved females from the USA with Maureen Connolly and Louise Brough winning the title three and four times respectively. In 1956 Britain's Angela Buxton broke the American monopoly by making it through to the last two (losing to Shirley Fry from Ohio), though it was business as usual again in 1957 when South Carolina's Althea Gibson and Darlene Hard of California contested the final. America's stranglehold on the competition was only broken with the arrival of Brazil's Maria Bueno who won Wimbledon in 1959, 1960 and again in 1964.

STEFFI'S PROPOSAL

Between 400,000 and 500,000 people attend the Wimbledon Championships every year. Almost inevitably a few of them will heckle players while they are busy competing, even in the holy confines of the Centre Court. One of the more memorable 'shouts' came during the 1996 Women's Singles semi-final between Steffi Graf and Kimiko Date of Japan. As Graf prepared to serve during the second set a young man's voice suddenly called out, 'Steffi! Will you marry me?' Quick as a flash Graf came back at him with the response, 'How much money do you have?' Not as much as Andre Agassi, clearly.

STUFF AND NONSENSE

Wimbledon can admittedly still seem a tad stuffy compared to, say, the 'anything goes' party atmosphere of the US Open. However, it's nothing like as bad as it used to be in days gone by. Just ask Jimmy Connors and Ilie Nastase. In 1975 the pair arrived together at the All England Club ahead of their respective second-round matches in the Men's Singles, only to be denied entry by a somewhat elderly gateman of military appearance. 'Why can't we go in?' asked the pair. 'Because it's not midday, and nobody's allowed in until then,' said the aloof gateman who proceeded to make two of the most famous sportsmen on the planet wait outside for five minutes until the Wimbledon clock finally struck 12. Days later Connors and Nastase, who had also joined forces in the Men's Doubles competition that year, were fined by the All England Club following a seemingly harmless prank involving one of their pairs matches. For a laugh the duo decided to take to Court 2 wearing rugby shirts bought from a local sports shop – Connors wearing the green of Ireland, Nastase the red of Wales. To top it all they donned bowler hats for the warm up. Why the fine? Because the pair had infringed Wimbledon's all-white dress code. Honestly. . . .

CALL ME

The life of a tennis professional can be a lonely one, negotiating a seemingly endless treadmill of airports, hotels and matches. Sometimes a player longs for a bit of, how shall I put it, 'company', to liven up the dead time in between competing. Pat Stewart appears to have been such a player. In 1961 the American took on Suzanne Chatrier in a second-round Women's Singles match with her telephone number plastered across her knickers for all to see, especially when bending forward to receive serve. Clearly her boldness didn't have the desired effect as Stewart repeated the stunt in the third round against Margaret Court, not that it did her on-court prospects any favours – she lost 6–3, 6–0.

THE 'OTHER' WIMBLEDON

On 12 January 2010 an earthquake measuring 7.3 on the Richter Scale hit the impoverished Caribbean country of Haiti, devastating the capital city Port-au-Prince. From the outset it was clear there were casualties on a massive scale with estimates putting the death toll at over 200,000. Almost immediately the international community swung into action with aid agencies making for Haiti initially to search for survivors and treat the injured. What's all this got to do with Wimbledon? Well one of those agencies was an organisation called Merlin, an acronym for 'Medical Emergency Relief International'. Merlin is a British charity dedicated to saving lives in times of crisis together with rebuilding shattered health infrastructures around the world. Within 36 hours of the earthquake striking, Merlin had set up a makeshift field hospital on some tennis courts in Delmas just outside Port-au-Prince. Over the coming weeks countless lives and limbs were saved at this hospital which acquired the nickname 'Wimbledon' both within medical circles and the local community, an indication if ever there was one of the tournament's global profile.

HAROLD'S HILL

Sadly all too many of the names mentioned on these pages departed this life horribly prematurely. Arthur Ashe, Maureen Connolly, Vitas Gerulaitis, Suzanne Lenglen, Tony Wilding . . . the list goes on. However, only one former Wimbledon Champion has met his maker through falling off a bicycle. His name was Harold Mahony, winner of the Men's Singles event in 1896, whose lifeless body was found lying across his mangled bike at the foot of Caragh Hill in County Kerry, Ireland, on 27 June 1905. He was 38 at the time of his death and had last competed at Wimbledon the previous year, losing in the third round to the Bristolian Frank Riseley.

FLOWER OF SCOTLAND

Although raised in Ireland, Harold Mahony was born in Edinburgh. Despite the arrival of brothers Jamie and Andy Murray on the scene, Scotland has never been what you might call fertile tennis territory. During the early 1970s one woman from north of the border did, however, manage to make a genuine impression on the world game. Born in Glasgow in 1947, Winnie Shaw won numerous British junior titles before turning professional during the mid-1960s. When tennis became 'Open' to all in 1968 Shaw became quite a force on the circuit, making the Wimbledon quarter-finals in both 1970 and 1971 when she lost to Rosie Casals and Margaret Court respectively. The following year Winnie was at it again, reaching the fourth round without dropping so much as a set where she had the misfortune to run into Billie Jean King, the all-conquering American prevailing 6–4, 6–2. Shaw was proud to be Scottish and never let anyone forget it. While playing a Federation Cup match for Britain in Greece, she twice took the umpire to task for referring to her as English. 'I'm Scottish and I'm representing Great Britain, not England,' she insisted firmly on both occasions. Sadly Shaw died of a brain tumour in 1992 aged only 45. She was inducted into the Scottish Sports Hall of Fame in 2002.

COINCIDENCE

One hundred and nineteen years to the day after Harold Mahony was born in Edinburgh (13 February 1867), Jamie Murray came into this world 43 miles away in the town of Dunblane (13 February 1986). As destiny would have it Murray duly became the next Scottish-born tennis player to win a senior Wimbledon title, partnering Jelena Jankovic of Serbia to glory in the Mixed Doubles event in 2007.

WIMBLEDON FINALE

More death I'm afraid, but on this occasion of a slightly more natural variety than earthquakes or bicycle crashes. Friends of Yorkshireman Colin Gregory used to joke that the only way he'd ever be prised away from Wimbledon would be in a box, such was his devotion to the place. Twice as a player he reached the quarter-finals of the Men's Singles at the All England

Club, losing to the eventual Champion Bill Tilden in 1930 having earlier disposed of a young Fred Perry. The previous year Gregory had made the final of the Men's Doubles with Scotland's Ian Collins, losing in five sets to the Americans Wilmer Allison and Johnny Van Ryn. Crowned the Australian Open Champion in 1929, he continued playing competitively into his forties appearing in a Davis Cup tie for Britain against Yugoslavia aged 48. In 1955 he was made chairman of the All England Club having been vice chairman for the previous four years. On 10 January 1959 Gregory had just finished playing a friendly game of doubles at Wimbledon with his son, daughter and close friend Dan Maskell when he suddenly collapsed and died of a heart attack in the dressing rooms. He was only 55 – far too young to go but, as the vast majority of those who attended his funeral service in Mortlake agreed, it couldn't have happened at a more appropriate place.

A PERFECT MATCH

At long last a tale with a happy ending. Tennis players, like most athletes, have their own pre-match rituals and preparation techniques such as what to eat for breakfast and how long to practise for. They appreciate the importance of those few hours immediately before a match, abiding by that old sporting adage that if you fail to prepare, then you may as well prepare to fail. In 1967 the South African player Cliff Drysdale went off on a tangent, and then some, when it came to his pre-match preparation ahead of a fourth-round Men's

Singles tie against Britain's Roger Taylor. That morning, instead of heading for the practice courts, Drysdale made for Paddington Registry Office where he married Jean Forbes, sister of his South African Davis Cup partner Gordon Forbes. Alas the magic of the moment failed to extend to the Centre Court where Taylor won in five sets to book his place in the quarter-finals.

IN A FIX

Up until recently tennis has got off relatively lightly when it comes to the sleazy side of sport, in particular the shadow cast by such unwanted intruders as drugs and match-fixing. However, only an eternal optimist wearing blinkers would doubt the lurking existence of both those demons on the circuit, especially the latter. Most national tennis governing bodies, including Britain's very own Lawn Tennis Association, now give briefings to young players about match-fixing – what to do if someone offers you money to throw a match or a particular set, the serious career implications of succumbing to temptation, etc. Ahead of Wimbledon 2009 it even became known that an official 'watch list' had been compiled by the sport's ruling authorities consisting of players under scrutiny for involvement in matches where suspicious betting patterns had been spotted. No names were mentioned, at least not publicly, but rumours abounded. All yours truly will say is that in 2006 I watched a match at Wimbledon involving two players – one from the southern hemisphere versus a European – where things just didn't seem right. But don't panic. The vast majority of tennis players are men and women of honour and integrity. Yet, as I said, only an eternal optimist would deny that a problem exists.

HANGING ON THE TELEPHONE

Times change as the years fly by, ushering in revolutionary ways of communicating. Today you can follow Wimbledon via several different methods, for instance on television, by listening to the extensive coverage on the radio, or perhaps best of all on the internet where the official Wimbledon website updates the scores of every match in progress on a point-by-point basis (even though you can't see the action, it's strangely hypnotic). As recently as the late 1970s, when many homes still didn't have TVs, the only way of receiving up-to-date news from Wimbledon was to call a telephone number at the All England Club – 01 483 8033 – which gave recorded information about results and matches in progress. For those without phones (and by that I mean landlines, not mobiles – this is the dark ages we're on about here) that meant a trip to the nearest public telephone box armed with a stack of 2p pieces to feed the thing. Archaic is the word – but nobody knew any better. And to think some people still insist that modern life is rubbish.

BJÖRN AGAIN

Ilie Nastase never won Wimbledon but with his notorious mood swings – joking around with a spectator one minute, throwing a tantrum about a dodgy line call the next – he was unquestionably one of the main draws around SW19 throughout the 1970s. The Romanian reached two Men's Singles finals, finishing runner-up to Stan Smith in 1972 and Björn Borg four years later. A couple of hours ahead of his first final, Nastase's friend Fred Perry arranged for him to have a practice session with an unknown 16-year-old who had reached the final of the Boys' Singles event. Nastase didn't know the kid from Adam but as Perry rated him highly that was a good enough letter of introduction. The pair hit for around 20 minutes on Court 4 at the All England Club before going their separate ways. The kid's name? Björn Borg.

ALL IN ONE

We're nearing the end of the *Miscellany* now and still the weather continues to cast its long shadow over the pages of this book. The 1999 Championships started off warm but gradually deteriorated to the point where the second Tuesday was completely washed out, play also being restricted on the Monday and Wednesday. Thankfully there was an improvement from Thursday onwards but the damage had been done. To cut a long(ish) story short the backlog of matches resulted in all five finals being played on the same day (Sunday), the first time this had happened in Wimbledon history. For the record Pete

Sampras and Lindsay Davenport beat Andre Agassi and Steffi Graf respectively to become the Singles Champions, all four having played their semi-final matches the previous day.

A THANKLESS TASK

Umpires and line judges (or rather line umpires to give them their proper title) are without doubt the unsung heroes of Wimbledon, receiving only scowls and abuse from players throughout the fortnight rather than any form of genuine thanks. That, my friends, is a sad indictment on the sport as officials are there not because they get paid well (they don't) but through a sheer love of tennis, many taking unpaid leave from work to oversee Wimbledon and other tournaments. Approximately 340 match officials cover the Championships each year of which 260, give or take a couple, are British. Chair umpires account for around 45 of the overall total, the remainder consisting of line judges and management staff. Chair umpires usually cover two matches per day while line judges (working in teams of nine for the show courts and seven for less high-profile courts) operate on a 75 minutes on, 75 minutes off basis. So what's the secret of judging whether a serve travelling at 140mph is in or out? Ask any line judge and they will say 'Watch the line, not the ball.' Fancy having a go yourself? First you need to be a member of the Association of British Tennis Officials (ABTO), so get onto them and see if you are made of the right stuff.

SOME SOUND ADVICE

Plenty of people are under the impression that getting into Wimbledon can be an expensive, difficult business. As regards entry, well it's not cheap. Prices have risen steeply since, say, the 1980s when a ground ticket granting access to the outside courts (and standing areas on the main show courts) would set you back around a fiver. The only way you can obtain a ticket as a matter of right is by being a member of the All England Club, a debenture holder or a council member of the Lawn Tennis Association. For mere mortals like us the best option is to belong to a tennis club affiliated to a county association (the latter distributes tickets among the former which are then divided between a few lucky members, often by way of a draw). Alternatively you could try applying direct to the All England Club for tickets issued through the Public Ballot, or simply turn up on the day (or 24 hours beforehand, just to be on the safe side) and join 'The Queue'. So what happens if you fork out big bucks and it rains? By and large the golden rule is this – should there be less than one hour's play due to rain, then you get a full refund. If there's more than one hour but less than two, you get 50 per cent of your money back. Sure, it all sounds like a lot of hassle but remember this – get into Wimbledon when the skies are blue and you will have a great time. As regards the best day to go, try either Wednesday or Thursday during the first week when the tournament is in full flow and there are still plenty of decent matches to see up-close on the outside courts. I promise you won't be disappointed.

FAMOUS LAST WORDS

'The one I'd like to win is Wimbledon. It's the intimacy, the exclusiveness of the club, how it's tucked away in a neighbourhood. It's not like New York where there's a huge stadium and it's, like, bam!'

Andy Roddick

'I went to watch when I was six and I remember thinking, "This is what I want. I want a piece of this."'

Tim Henman recalls his first visit to Wimbledon

'I often surprise myself. You can't plan some shots that go in, not unless you're on marijuana, and the only grass I'm partial to is Wimbledon's.'

Rod Laver

'If you put two monkeys on to play you'd still pack the Centre Court.'

Neil Fraser on Wimbledon's popularity

'To be out there is the greatest feeling in the world.'

Andre Agassi on the Centre Court

'God, yeah – Wimbledon is still the big one!'

Pat Rafter